SAFE AND EFFECTIVE WORKOUTS *for* SENIORS

Printed in America

ISBN – Paperback : 979-8-9894378-0-1

MY GIFT TO YOU!

Just My Way of Saying Thank You

Completely FREE

Scan the QR Code Below to Download

https://fallproof.aweb.page/

CONTENTS

INTRODUCTION 13

Why I wrote this book 14

Who is this book for? 18

What does this book include? 18

What is your "why"? 20

PART I: OUR BODY AND THE AGING PROCESS 23

CHAPTER 1: WHY DON'T WE EXERCISE? 25

Myth 1: I'm getting old anyway; what's the point? 26

Myth 2: Exercise puts me at risk of falling. 26

Myth 3: It's too frustrating; I'll never be the athlete I used to be. 27

Myth 4: I'm too old to start exercising. 28

Myth 5: I can't exercise because I'm disabled. 28

Myth 6: I'm too weak to exercise. 29

Myth 7: I have too many aches and pains. 29

Myth 8: I don't like to exercise. 30

CHAPTER 2: WHAT IS HAPPENING TO MY BODY? 31

Your Skeleton 31

Your Joints 32

Your Muscles 32

Your Ligaments and Tendons 33

Your Circulation and Heart 34

Your Bladder and Urinary Tract 34

Your Memory and Cognitive Skills 35

Your Posture 35

Your Balance 36

Your Weight Gain and Loss 37

CHAPTER 3: WHAT ARE THE BEST TYPES OF EXERCISES FOR SENIORS? 39

Pillar I – Building Strength 41

Pillar II – Increasing Flexibility 42

Pillar III – Improving Balance 43
Pillar IV – Building Endurance 45
CHAPTER 4: WHAT ARE OUR MAJOR MUSCLES? 48
Your Upper Body Muscles 48
Your Core Muscles 52
Your Lower Body Muscles 56
CHAPTER 5: HOW TO TAILOR YOUR EXERCISE PROGRAM TO YOU 59
Know Your Body 60
Overweight 61
Arthritis 63
Osteoporosis or Osteopenia 65
Diabetes 67
CHAPTER 6: ALWAYS PUT SAFETY FIRST 73
Safety Considerations 73
Talk to Your Doctor 77
CHAPTER 7: WHAT ABOUT EQUIPMENT? 78
A Sturdy Chair 79
Light Weights 80
Small Balls 82
Other Items 83
CHAPTER 8: IT'S YOUR CHOICE 84
How Do You Stay Motivated? 86
When All Else Fails 91
PART II: LET'S EXERCISE 95
CHAPTER 9: TERMINOLOGY AND NOTATIONS 97
Standard Terminology 97
Exercise Notations 100
Other Notes 102
CHAPTER 10: BUILDING STRENGTH 104
Strength Training – Upper Body 106

Shoulder Raises 106
Shoulder Squeeze 108
Rotator Cuff Strengthen 110
Seated Push-Back 112
Dumbbell Row 114
Push Back 116
Arm Lifts 118
Chest Extension 120
Bicep Curl 122
Bicep Strengthening 124
Triceps Curl 126
Triceps Push 128
Elbow Extensions 130
STRENGTH TRAINING – CORE 132
Diaphragmatic Breathing 132
Pelvic Floor Kegels 135
Dolphin Kick 141
Leg Extension 143
Dead Bug 145
Reverse Crunch 147
Plank 149
Bridge 151
Extended Bridge 153
Clam 155
Side Leg Lift 157
Flutter Kick 159
STRENGTH BUILDING – LOWER BODY 161
Modified Heel Drops 161
Inner Thigh Lifts 163
Outer Thigh Lifts 165
Seated March 167
Wall Squats 169
Seated Leg Lifts 171
Standing Heel Raises 173
Rolling Ball Massage 175

Tiptoe Walking 177
Ankle Flex 179
Toe Grabs 181

CHAPTER 11: INCREASING FLEXIBILITY 183

DYNAMIC STRETCHES – WARM- UP EXERCISES...186
March in Place 186
Squats..187
Walking Lunge 189
Arm Circles 190
Shoulder Blade Squeeze 191
Punches...192
STATIC STRETCHES - UPPER BODY 193
Neck Flex 193
Neck Extension 194
Neck Side Flexion 195
Neck Rotation 196
Chin Tuck...197
Shoulder Stretch..198
Overhead Stretch 199
Elbow Wrap Stretch 200
Standing Chest Expansion..201
Shoulder Shrug..202
Shoulder Pull 203
Chest Expansion 204
Upper Back Stretch 205
Upper Back Extension...206
Wrist and Forearm Flex /Down..207
Flex Up...208
Squeeze the Ball 210
Finger Spread 212
Thumb Press..214
STATIC STRETCHES – LOWER BODY 215
Lower Back Extension...215
Lower Back Side Flex 217
Hamstring Stretch 218

Thigh Pull Stretch 219
Figure Four Stretch 220
Seated Hamstring 221
Standing Quad Stretch 222
Seated Glute Stretch 223
Seated Hip Stretch 224
Standing Hip Stretch 225
Standing Calf Stretch 226

CHAPTER 12: IMPROVING BALANCE 227

BALANCE EXERCISES 229
Three-Way Toe Tap 229
Side-to-Side 231
Sit to Stand 233
Wall Press 235
Stand on One Foot 237
Heel Raises 239
Toe Raises 241

CHAPTER 13: BUILDING ENDURANCE 243

Cycling 244
Swimming 244
Dancing 245
Walking 246

CHAPTER 14: PULLING IT ALL TOGETHER 249

CREATE YOUR OWN EXERCISE PROGRAM 250
FOUR WEEK AGELESS AGILITY EXERCISE PROGRAM 254
A CAUTION ABOUT OVEREXERCISING 256

APPENDIX I: DYNAMIC (WARM-UP) STRETCHES 259

APPENDIX II: CREATE YOUR OWN EXERCISE PROGRAM 263

APPENDIX III: 4-WEEK AGELESS AGILITY EXERCISE PROGRAMS 277

SOURCES 315

SAFE AND EFFECTIVE WORKOUTS *for* SENIORS

JO MARQUES

INTRODUCTION

Hi, my name is Jo. I am 73 years of age, which, based on society's definition, puts me squarely in the age range considered to be a "senior." I must admit that I don't care for that classification. Somehow, being designated “a senior” also subtlety implies that you (if you are 60 or older) and I are in that age range where we are experiencing, or could expect to experience, a decline in our physical capabilities and perhaps mental sharpness. It implies a time when we are expected to do less and maybe even live a less fulfilled life. For some, hitting this age means thinking about how long they can live independently.

So, when the subject of aging has come up with friends or family, I have always laughed and given one of my favorite sayings: "Don't you know that 70 is the new 50?" or, "Age is just a number, and I am in denial" or, "I'm siding with Abraham Lincoln, who said 'it is not the years in your life that count, it's the life in your years.'" As the 16th President of the United States, old Abe must have known what he was talking about.

It isn't that I don't recognize and acknowledge that with aging comes some decline in our physical and mental capabilities. I have certainly experienced these and continue to do so. I just believe we are better served to focus on what a wonderful time this is in our lives. It is a time where the significant stresses of our jobs and careers should be behind us, a time when our families have grown and hopefully are on their own, a time where the lessons we have learned along life's journey can be leveraged to help others, a time when we can play with our grandchildren, travel with a loved one, garden, play golf, or be able to do whatever we enjoy doing. These are supposed to be our "Golden Years."

But, if our "Golden Years" will indeed be "Golden," we need to be physically able to enjoy them. That means we must accept our role and responsibility for ensuring we are as physically capable as our current health situation allows.

This book is about showing you how to do that.

Why I wrote this book

In my early 60s, I developed an autoimmune disease that affected my muscles. Although the condition is mostly under control, it has weakened my legs permanently and limited the types of exercise I can do. I have never really liked to exercise, so this seemed like an excellent excuse to do less and less as the years went by. I still enjoyed walking with friends, shopping, and being generally active, but I did less and less exercise.

Then COVID came. Mentally, I may be in the 50-year age group, but my body is still in the 70-year age group. My age and underlying health condition put me squarely in the high-risk zone for getting sick or even facing death. So, for over two years, I stayed indoors and did very little activity. I read, watched TV, surfed the internet, called friends and family, and ate. Since I could no longer join my friends for walks, shopping, or outings, this was another reason not to exercise.

When it was time to emerge and regain some resemblance to pre-COVID life, I found that I had gained 20 pounds and lost a lot of flexibility and strength. My balance was just horrible. The adage, "If you don't use it, you lose it," was becoming true for me. For the first time since I officially became a "senior," I was beginning to feel like I was getting old! I was always tired, had little energy, my knee hurt, and I couldn't walk far without pain.

My wake-up call came when I went on a long overdue trip to see my son, daughter-in-law, and four beautiful grandchildren. One of the things I enjoy most is visiting my family and enjoying the fun things we do together. As soon as I arrive, we are always off to an activity. This time, however, it was very different. I was so out of shape that I couldn't keep up with them, much less actively participate. We took the younger children to the Atlanta Aquarium and had to park a few blocks away. It was difficult for me to walk that far, so I found excuses to stop momentarily and look at some flowers or another distraction to rest a bit. The Aquarium is on two levels, connected by beautifully designed stairways. When it was time to walk up, I found myself thinking, "I don't think I can walk up that far." I jokingly told my family to head on up and that I would meet them there in a few minutes. Then, I found the nearest elevator. Suddenly it hit me that my famous motto of "70 is the new 50" would no longer be true if I couldn't remain mobile.

It got worse when we visited another attraction that used a moving sidewalk with a slight incline and no handrails. I stepped on only to find that I couldn't maintain my balance, and I fell. The sidewalk was stopped, but I couldn't get myself up without something to grab onto, and I needed help. I was embarrassed and frightened!

The final straw came when my son and I discussed a vacation trip planned for later in the year to Universal Studios in Orlando, Florida. My son said, "Mom, don't worry if you can't walk around that much. We will get a wheelchair and push you!" In my head, I was screaming, "NO! NO! NO! I can't let this happen!"

I was at a crossroads. The moment of decision was staring me in the face. First, I could continue my "I have never liked to exercise" excuse, which would most likely result in spending my "Golden Years" sitting in a chair, possibly even a wheelchair, and watching my family from a distance. Second, I could get off the sofa and start an exercise program to rebuild my strength, flexibility, balance, and endurance. I chose to do everything I could to ensure I had the physical capacity to enjoy this special time in my life. This book is the result of my decision.

After returning home, I immediately got to work on the new, stronger, more flexible, more mobile me. I was determined to find a way to improve my physical capability so that I could fully participate in and enjoy the next outing with my grandchildren. Thus began a deep dive into research on how to do this. I read and studied material by leading health experts and met with physical therapists, doctors, and experts in the field. I bought courses and tried different exercise programs. I got off the couch and got moving. As a result, I've greatly improved my strength, flexibility, balance, and stamina.

We all know that exercise alone is not the only factor in how well we age. There are also other important factors, such as:

- Attitude
- Diet
- Personal Habits such as Smoking, Drinking, and Taking Other Harmful Substances
- Socialization or Lack Thereof
- Stress and Anxiety
- Other Health Issues
- Mental Health
- Side Effects of Prescribed Medication

These all play a significant role and are areas you may want to include in your general wellness plan. This book, however, is dedicated to helping you improve your physical fitness, which is vital to healthy aging.

Writing this book became my passion. I am dedicated to ensuring that I am the most youthful, active, strong, and mobile 70-plus-year-old I can be. I am excited about sharing this information with you and helping you become the very best version of yourself.

Who is this book for?

The exercises in this book are tailored to:

- The Beginner – You may not have exercised much before or have never exercised.
- The Reluctant – You may not like to exercise.
- The Recuperating – You may be recovering from an illness or injury.
- The Chronic Illness Sufferer – You may be limited in the types of exercises you can do.
- The Active – You may be in reasonably good physical shape and want to retain and expand your balance, flexibility, strength, and stamina.

What does this book include?

This book includes vital information on how and why we age and provides exercises addressing many common issues. These exercises have been reviewed by a medical professional and are safe to do, subject, of course, to your doctor's consent, if you have:

- Osteoporosis
- Osteopenia
- Arthritis or Joint Issues
- Diabetes
- Autoimmune Disease
- A Weight Problem

They will help you to:

- Build Muscle Mass
- Expand Flexibility.
- Correct Balance Issues
- Increase Endurance

The exercises and exercise programs are flexible and include:

- Instructions – Each exercise includes detailed illustrations and simple, easy-to-follow instructions.
- Muscle Groups – There are exercises for each major muscle group in your body.
- Ramp-Up Option – Most exercises include a "Ramp-Up" option to challenge you after you have mastered the basic routine.
- Cautions – Most exercises include a "Caution" section to provide options to scale back the exercise if it is too difficult for you now.
- Seated, Standing, or Lying Down – Exercises for each position are included so you can select what position is best for you.

- Weights – some of the exercises recommend the use of light weights and other no cost or inexpensive equipment.
- Fit Fun Exercises – many of the exercises are identified as "FIT FUN," which means they can easily fit into your day while watching TV, cooking, or doing other normal daily living functions.
- Flexible Exercise Programs – You can select the "Create Your Own" Program or the "Four Week Ageless Agility" exercise program.

For ease of use, this book is divided into two sections:

- Part I discusses our bodies and how the natural process of aging affects us. It focuses on how to safely build vitality and slow aging, even with age-related physical constraints.
- Part II includes easy-to-follow exercises designed to help you safely build strength, increase flexibility, improve your balance, and build endurance. If you want to go immediately to the exercises, jump to Part II.

What is your "why"?

This book contains a great deal of information you can use to improve your physical condition. But first, it is essential to take a moment to think about WHY you are reading this book. I have shared my reason with you.

What about you?

- Are you tired all the time?
- Are you starting to have balance issues and are afraid of falling?
- Have you felt a decrease in your overall strength and flexibility?
- Do you have dreams and goals that you want to achieve that require physical capability?
- Do you want to continue doing the things that you love?
- Do you want to delay or avoid going into an assisted living facility or relying on your family for help?

Wouldn't it be wonderful if reading about something and wishing it would happen would make it happen? Sadly, that is not the case.

Starting any new program or changing a pattern in your life requires change. And starting a new exercise program is no different. Beginning this, or any other new program, will require new habits, new disciplines, and a new or revived commitment to your health. Change is easier if you are clear on what you want to achieve and, most importantly, WHY you want to make it happen.

Take a moment now and jot down on the next page:

What is your WHY?

I want to take responsibility for my health and physical vitality because

____

____

____

____

____

____

____

____

Let's get started!

PART I

OUR BODY AND THE AGING PROCESS

WHY EXERCISE IS IMPORTANT

CHAPTER 1

WHY DON'T WE EXERCISE?

Most of us know that we should be exercising. We have probably heard more than one doctor's lecture about the importance of exercise and why we need to start doing it. Most of us have seen the advertisements on TV or read articles in the latest senior magazine touting the importance of exercise. We most likely have read about studies, such as the one recently conducted in Sweden, showing physical activity and exercise is the number one contributor to seniors' longevity and quality of life.

So, why is it that even though medical research has shown that exercise is good for us, only about 25% of people between the ages of 65 and 75 actively exercise, and the statistics drop to only 11% for people aged 85 years and older? If you are in this group, like I was, ask yourself why. Have you "bought into" one of the common myths about senior exercising?

Let's examine those.

Myth 1: I'm getting old anyway; what's the point?

The real question is: How fast do you want to age? It is probably safe to say that most of us would like to slow down that process as much as possible. None of us want to be sick, in a wheelchair, or unable to care for ourselves. We all want to be as healthy and independent for as long as we possibly can. We do not have any control over the fact that we are aging, nor do we have any control over the date and time when we will be called from this life. However, we have some control over how we live life now. We do have some control over what we will be doing when that final time comes; that is, will we be weak and forced to live with the round-the-clock care that comes with a nursing home, or will we be on the tennis court or doing something else we love.

Medical communities and numerous well-documented studies have proven it. Regular exercise can slow aging and give seniors many years of active and independent living. So, "What's the point?" The "point" is that exercise can allow us to slow the aging process, and it can help us have the physical capability to enjoy an active and independent lifestyle.

Myth 2: Exercise puts me at risk of falling.

It is true that as we age, our balance often gets worse, and with that can come a real fear of falling. The question is, will we accept this and allow our balance issue and our fear of falling to control the rest of our lives, or will we do something to improve our balance?

The Journal of Clinical Medicine published a paper in August 2020 on research investigating the effect of exercise on senior's balance. The study concluded that "physical exercise is an effective treatment to improve balance and reduce the number of falls for patients aged 65 or over."

When you start doing balance exercises, you may be unsteady and need to hold onto something to stabilize yourself. You may even need to start lying on the bed or sitting down, but your muscles will become stronger as you continue to exercise. As your muscles strengthen, they become more flexible. Greater flexibility means your body is more fluid and can counteract the forces of gravity more quickly and efficiently. Stronger muscles also mean better coordination, which directly influences how you walk and move. The more coordinated your body is, the less likely you are to trip or stumble. The result is better balance and a lower risk of falling.

Myth 3: It's too frustrating; I'll never be the athlete I used to be.

Let's face it: at this point in our lives, none of us have the physical capabilities to be the athletes we were in our youth. But you have a head start in being the best athlete you can be now. Because muscles have memory, you can build strength and muscle mass quicker than someone who has never exercised. You can still derive a sense of achievement and pride in your physical abilities. The key is to set goals appropriate for your age and ability and then strive to achieve these.

Myth 4: I'm too old to start exercising.

So, let me share a fact with you: You are never too old to start exercising. Medical research supports this. The real benefit of improving your general health will be evident when you start exercising. Start slowly at the lowest level and gradually work your way through to the more challenging "ramp-up" exercises. Just be realistic about your level of fitness and your capability.

Myth 5: I can't exercise because I'm disabled.

As we age, we can experience physical limitations and perhaps even disabilities. I have a condition that has affected my leg muscle. You may also have an underlying condition that makes exercise difficult. You may need to work with these challenges, but they don't need to be challenges that stop you. Just start where you are and do what you can for now. Look through this book and find the exercises you can do while sitting in a chair or lying on your bed. Focus on these exercises and then slowly build from this point onward. After you have mastered these exercises, look for another two or three to add to your routine. The important thing is that you are moving forward.

Myth 6: I'm too weak to exercise.

If you are weak now, unfortunately, you will continue to get weaker without exercise. Exercise builds strength and endurance. If you start where you are and do a little exercise or stretching each day, it won't take long before you can do much more, not only in increased exercise but also in your everyday life. Start with one or two easy exercises and try a few repetitions.

Repeat for a few days and add another exercise or additional repetitions. Set a goal to walk for 10 minutes after dinner. What matters is that you take some action to rebuild your strength.

Myth 7: I have too many aches and pains.

It is a fact of life: as we age, our bodies change, often bringing a host of aches and pains. It is easier to take the comfortable route and allow those body aches to rob us of activity. By not exercising, we are just bringing ourselves more aches and pains as muscles waste away and joints, ligaments, and bones are no longer supported.

So again, you must ask yourselves, "Am I going to let the normal aches and pains that come with aging rob me of the joy that this time in my life can bring?" If the answer is no, start slowly and gently, but start. You'll be so glad you did when, in a few short weeks, the aches and pains should begin to fade away.

Myth 8: I don't like to exercise.

Not liking to exercise is not so much a myth as a personal like or dislike. As I mentioned earlier, I didn't like to exercise either. But I disliked the results of not exercising even more. I disliked being unable to play with my grandchildren or participate in family outings. I disliked not being able to keep up with friends. The question I had to answer (and if this is your issue, you must also answer) is, "What do you dislike more: a few hours a week exercising or not being able to live life as you want fully?" If you want to live your life fully, then I encourage you to find ways of exercising that you'll find fun. We will talk more about this later in Chapter 8.

It is time to bury these myths and replace them with facts. It is time to start your journey to a stronger and more physically capable you. You'll be so glad that you did!

CHAPTER 2

WHAT IS HAPPENING TO MY BODY?

Have you found that your body is no longer behaving as it used to? Perhaps you're not quite as tall as before, or your usually strong fingers show signs of weakness and stiffness. Keeping your balance may be becoming more challenging, or it may take longer to get moving. Have you ever thought, "What is happening to me?" Let's talk about what happens to our bodies as we age.

Your Skeleton

The spine, at the center of the body, has bones called vertebrae linked together by cushioning discs. The bones of our heads, arms, and legs are attached to our spine. The bones are comprised of bone cells and connective tissue, which are strengthened by calcium and phosphate. When we are young, the skeleton constantly builds up new bone tissue as the old bone tissue breaks down. But, as we age, the renewing process slows down, and the body reabsorbs the calcium and phosphate, which results in weaker bones and can lead to osteoporosis. Osteoporosis is a dangerous condition that can result in falls and serious injury.

Exercise can help - strength-building exercises can increase our bone mass and, if caught soon enough, can prevent the onset of osteoporosis.

Your Joints

As we age, connective tissue and cartilage between the bones that generally provide cushioning wear down, and the fluid decreases. With reduced fluid in the joints, the ends of the bones may begin to rub together, causing inflammation and stiffness. As the cartilage wears away, the discomfort and pain increase. Sometimes, there is also a deposit of minerals due to higher uric acid levels, which causes spurs to form, increasing the pain and compromising the joint's movement.

Exercise can help - arthritic joints benefit from exercise. Exercise can alleviate pressure on the nerves and restore flexibility and strength, making moving easier. Maintaining the tone of the muscles keeps them strong and helps to support the joints.

Your Muscles

As we progress through the different stages of our lives, our muscle mass and strength also go through cycles of change. Typically, our strength and muscle capacity increase steadily from the time we are born until we are around age 30 to 35, when it tends to peak. After that, we typically experience a slow but steady decline in our muscle performance. That decline increases in women after the age of 65 and in men after the age of 70.

As a result, seniors often develop sarcopenia, defined as a decline in muscle mass, strength, and function. Sarcopenia is connected to weakness, fatigue, and lower energy levels, resulting in difficulty standing, walking, and climbing stairs. People with sarcopenia are at risk for falls, fractures, serious injuries, and even premature mortality.

Exercise can help - research has proven that strength or weight training can slow the process as it builds bone and muscle mass. Stronger muscles mean better balance and greater stability.

Your Ligaments and Tendons

As joints get compromised, and muscles weaken, the ligaments and tendons are put under strain. Calcium deposits in these soft tissues can also make them less flexible and hard to stretch, causing the body to be less mobile.

Exercise can help - our body works as a unit; thus, exercising and strengthening muscles will take the strain off the ligaments and tendons and improve flexibility and stability.

Your Circulation and Heart

As we age, it is common to find that our blood vessels stiffen and harden, which makes our hearts work harder to pump blood around our bodies. High blood pressure and other heart issues can result.

Exercise can help - according to the American College of Sports Medicine and The American Heart Association, activity, and in particular aerobic exercise, combined with strength-building exercises, helps to improve circulation. An added benefit is improved oxygen flow to the muscles and bones. Walking, swimming, bicycle riding, and weight-bearing exercises are all excellent. These types of exercise decrease the risk of heart disease.

Your Bladder and Urinary Tract

Urinary incontinence is often associated with aging. This embarrassing condition can result in leaking if we cough, sneeze, bend, or do any aerobic activity. It is usually caused by weakening pelvic floor muscles and a bladder that is not as elastic as it was in our youth. There can be further complications in men by the prostate becoming enlarged or inflamed. Other complications that affect urinary continence are overweight, nerve damage, and certain medications.

Exercise can help - unless a medical issue causes the incontinence, regular exercise can help reduce urinary incontinence and erectile problems. Low-impact exercises can help to strengthen core abdominal muscles. Other exercises to elongate the spine and lift the chest muscles will also help. Kegel exercises can strengthen the pelvic floor muscles.

Your Memory and Cognitive Skills

As we age, our brain cells undergo normal changes that can affect our memory. We may forget names or lose our keys more often. Multi-tasking may be more difficult than it used to be. These are normal changes unrelated to Alzheimer's disease or dementia, which have a story of their own.

Exercise can help - research from Harvard shows exercise can help boost our thinking skills and maintain the health of existing brain cells. Many studies have shown that in people who exercise, the part of the brain that controls thinking and memory is slightly larger than in people who don't exercise.

Even more exciting is the finding that engaging in a program of regular exercise of moderate intensity over six months or a year is associated with an increase in the volume of selected brain regions.

Your Posture

Have you noticed that friends around your age are getting shorter? You may have noticed that the hems of your pants are too long. You may be wondering if you've shrunk. As we age, we lose about a half to a three-quarter inch (1,2–1,9 cm) in height.

Several factors cause this:

- Shoulders are more rounded, causing the head to tilt forward.
- Vertebral discs are losing fluid and flattening or shrinking, resulting in compression and shortening.
- Foot arches slacken and become less pronounced.
- Weight gain collects in the front or tummy area, pulling the spine forward and putting pressure on the lower back.

Exercise can help - exercising the upper body helps strengthen your back, neck, and shoulders by toning these crucial muscles, enables you to stand more upright, and counteracts the stoop that accounts for much of the "loss" in height. Keep your posture in mind as you go about your day. Focus on pulling in the tummy muscles and standing up straight.

Even this simple activity will help a lot. By the way, this hunched forward position can also impact your breathing, balance, and ability to cope with daily tasks that require stretching your arms upward.

Your Balance

Several factors can cause balance issues. A prevalent cause is aging and its effect on our bones, muscles, and joints. Weak bones, muscles, and joints typically also mean poor balance. Loss of vision, drop in blood pressure or blood sugar, inner ear problems, neuropathy, or a reaction to a medication can also cause balance issues. If you feel your poor balance may be caused by one of these issues, consult your medical professional.

If the cause of your balance issue is the age-related weakening of your musculoskeletal system, then the correct type of exercise can help.

Your Weight Gain and Loss

As we get older, most of us tend to gain weight. Decreased activity plus continuing to have the same or increased food intake is often the cause. That excess fat seems to sit around our middle, and if you have ever had a weight issue, you know it is hard to lose. The result is that many of us end up with a rounded middle section and skinny limbs.

Some individuals tend to lose weight as they age. Men can gain weight until age 55 and women until age 65, but the picture can change afterward. Since the bulk of our weight comes from bone and muscle mass, which starts to decrease, weight loss can occur. In males, this is also due to a drop in the male hormone testosterone.

Exercise can help - If you are trying to lose weight, exercise can help maintain muscle mass and burn fat. Less fat means a leaner trimmer you. If you are losing weight because of decreased muscle mass, exercise can help you rebuild your muscle mass, which can help you reach your ideal weight.

Knowledge Is Powerful

At this point, this may all sound a bit depressing. I know.

I felt that way at first. But ignoring this information or pretending it isn't happening will not stop the natural aging process. Having the correct knowledge and deciding to take action can slow the process and contribute to a longer, healthier, more active life.

The facts are:

Fact: Aging is a normal part of life. If we live long enough, we will all experience the aches, pains, and muscular declines that come with each passing chronological year.

Fact: Exercise and physical activity can slow the impact of aging on our bodies. According to a recent study, physical activity is the main contributing factor to improving quality of life and increasing lifespan.

Fact: We have a choice. We can choose to sit back and let the aging process take its natural course, or we can decide to do everything we can to slow that process and build greater strength, flexibility, stamina, and balance so that we can maximize our ability to enjoy this special time in our lives.

CHAPTER 3

WHAT ARE THE BEST TYPES OF EXERCISES FOR SENIORS?

Medical professionals tell us that we need four types of exercise to maintain a strong, flexible, healthy body. These exercises improve strength, increase flexibility, improve balance, and build endurance. Each of these contributes to our overall level of fitness.

Consider the award-winning Pont Jacques Chaban-Delmas bridge in Bordeaux, France.

The Pont Jacques Chaban-Delmas bridge is the longest vertical lift bridge in Europe. It spans 2,220 feet over the Garonne River and is 252 feet high. Four slender pillars or pylons support this sturdy and impressive structure. Without each of these supporting pillars, there would be no bridge.

Like the Pont Jacques Chaban-Delmas bridge, our body is also an amazing structure. We can think of our bodies as the bridge that enables us to reach our desired destinations and engage in our favorite activities. Our exercise program should also focus on four pillars of exercise to ensure our bodies have the physical capability to take us where we want to go.

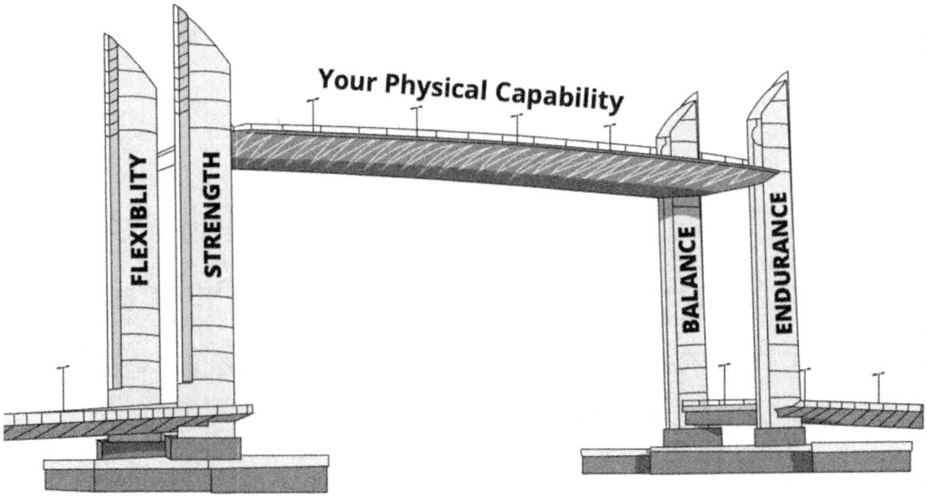

Pillar I – Building Strength

We need strength to perform the normal activities of daily living. We want to be able to pick up small grandchildren, manage a 45–50-pound suitcase to travel, carry groceries from the store to the car and from the car to the kitchen, grip and twist the lid to a jar of our favorite jam, lift a laundry basket of clothes, and so on. Strength-building exercises maintain and rebuild muscle mass and prevent bone density loss. They help increase the speed of our physical reactions to prevent us from falling.

Research done at Tufts University in Middlesex County, Massachusetts, showed that when done regularly, strength or weight training builds bones and muscle, helps preserve independence and strength, and increases energy.

The study concluded that people with health concerns such as arthritis and heart disease benefitted from lifting moderate weights a few times per week. It also found that participation in a moderate strength-building program reduced the signs and symptoms of many chronic conditions, such as:

- Arthritis – pain and stiffness are reduced, and strength and flexibility increase.
- Osteoporosis – bone density is built, and there are fewer bone breaks.
- Diabetes – glycemic control is improved.

- Heart disease – the lipid profile is reduced, and overall fitness improves.
- Overweight - the metabolism increases, and more calories are burned, helping to control weight.
- Back pain – as abdominal muscles strengthen, stress is reduced on the spine, and pain levels are lowered.
- Mental and emotional health – positivity and mood improve when strength training is done with aerobic exercise.
- Sleep – seniors who exercise regularly can sleep more deeply, for more extended periods, and wake less often at night.

Pillar II – Increasing Flexibility

Flexibility allows us to do everyday activities such as putting on our socks and shoes, turning our heads to look behind us, bending down to pick up a child's toy, or reaching up to get something out of the cabinet. Having adequate flexibility is essential to maintaining an active, independent lifestyle. Stretching exercises increase flexibility.

The Journal of Exercise, Sports, and Orthopedics recently reported on a study of older active adults aged 67–80 who performed stretches five times a week for over a year. They found that, on average, these seniors experienced a 31% increase in flexibility and a 10–17% increase in muscle strength. The test group also found that static stretching released muscle stress and tension.

Stretching can also:

- Improve your posture – when you stretch your neck, shoulders, back, and chest, you also improve your spine's alignment, which means better posture.
- Alleviate lower back pain and sciatic nerve pinches – stretching keeps your hip flexors, hamstrings, glutes, and other muscles in the pelvic region flexible.
- Improve your range of motion – stretching slows down the process of joint deterioration and the resulting limitation to your range of motion.
- Keep your blood circulation well-oxygenated – thus helping you maintain general health and your ability to fight off disease.
- Reduce your risk of falling – your muscles are more flexible, and you will be able to catch yourself more quickly if you start to fall.

Pillar III – Improving Balance

As we age, balance issues and the fear of falling become very real. I shared my fall experience earlier in the book. You may have fallen or have friends or family members who have fallen and suffered the consequences. If we are lucky and flexible enough to catch ourselves as we fall, we may end up with only bruises and a painful body for a few days. If we are not, the injuries could be severe and even life-threatening.

Consider these alarming statistics:

- Every 11 seconds, someone over 60 in the USA falls, which results in a trip to the emergency room.
- One in every three people over 65 dies from a fall. It's not always a direct result of the fall itself but could be from the residual effects over the prevailing weeks, months, and years.
- According to the research, if you fall more than twice in one year, your risk of more severe consequences (even death) within the next five years increases by over 200%.
- If you do slip and fall, according to the data, your chances of winding up in a nursing home triple.
- On a positive note, the statistics also show that seniors who exercise recover more quickly from minor falls than their peers who do not exercise.

Here are some benefits of improving balance:

- It minimizes the need to compensate – have you ever noticed a friend or older family member with skewed shoulders, one higher than the other? Skewed shoulders happen when muscles on one side of the body are more toned than the other, and we subconsciously compensate for the weaker side. Doing exercise to improve balance will ensure that muscles on both sides of the body are equally toned, improving posture.
- Improves core stability – having a stable core through doing exercises means that our body is balanced at the "center" or core, decreasing our risk of falling and improving our posture and, therefore, our balance.

- Improves flexibility of muscles – think of a flexible ruler and how it "bounces" back if you try to bend it a little, in contrast to a rigid plastic one that will snap when bent. It's the same with our muscles. Our bodies can "bounce back to position" without falling if they are more flexible.
- Minimizes the risk of falling – stronger muscles mean more confident movements, leading to less overbalancing and fewer falls.
- Improves coordination – our body needs good balance for coordination. Exercises that improve balance will automatically have a positive effect on coordinating our body movements. If both sides of our body are coordinated when we get out of a chair, for example, there is less likely to be a strain on the weaker side, possibly resulting in a fall.

Pillar IV – Building Endurance

We need endurance to give us the energy and "pep in our step" to get us through the day enjoyably. Endurance is that beautiful energy that allows us to play with our grandchildren without feeling wiped out or plan excursions with our friends and family without fear of slowing them down. For some of us, it may even give us the confidence to plan that two-week safari we have always dreamed of or travel halfway around the world to see an architectural wonder. Developing our endurance means that we'll be able to do more. It means we can "keep going" for longer and are doing what we can to actively push away frailty.

Endurance exercises are often called aerobic exercises because they increase our breathing and heart rate. These exercises improve the health of our hearts, lungs, and circulatory systems, and they can also prevent or delay health issues, such as heart disease, diabetes, cancers, and others that often occur as we age.

Adding endurance training into your exercise routine can provide the following benefits:

- Enhanced metabolism – lean muscle boosts metabolism by combating the natural slowing of age.
- A healthier body – endurance training strengthens the cardiorespiratory function, providing more power to the muscles of the heart and lungs. Better circulation means healthier bones and joints and increased muscle mass.
- It clears our thoughts – improved blood flow to the brain helps with cognitive ability. It helps to retard the onset of Alzheimer's disease to a degree.
- Increases self-confidence – the more you can do due to increased energy, the more confident you will feel. When simple tasks become difficult due to a lack of endurance, one loses confidence in one's ability. Endurance training helps increase your ability to do things and follow through.
- Improves sleep quality – endurance training keeps the body energized and refreshed and the lungs functioning well. A good air supply means better sleep.

- Keeps us feeling younger – the human growth hormone is linked to endurance training and has several health benefits, including anti-aging.
- Boosts the immune system – we can fight germs and bacteria more effectively. Seniors who do endurance training get sick less often; if they get sick, they recover quicker because increased oxygen levels through circulation increase the production of white blood cells and antibodies.
- Helps to control blood glucose levels – our body stores glucose in the muscles. Increased muscle mass allows for greater storage, taking pressure off the pancreas by decreasing the demand made on insulin production.

CHAPTER 4

WHAT ARE OUR MAJOR MUSCLES?

If you want to know more about the muscles we will work and their role in your overall well-being, this chapter is for you. On the other hand, if this level of detail tends to make your "eyes glaze over," you may want to skip this chapter and proceed directly to the next.

For this book, the primary muscles have been grouped into three categories: the upper body muscles, the core muscles, and the lower body muscles. The accompanying anatomical illustrations provide a visual of each muscle group's location in the body.

Your Upper Body Muscles

The upper body muscles include the neck, shoulders, chest, arms, forearms, hands, fingers, and the major upper/middle back muscles. All these muscles must be strong to give you a good range of motion for daily living. They connect the chest, limbs, and torso to your spinal column and control:

- The strength of your grasp, clenching of your fingers, and your hold on objects.
- Your ability to push, pull, and press with your arms, shoulders, back, and chest.
- Your range of motion, including ensuring you can move your arms in all directions.
- Your ability to extend your hands, flex your wrists, and move your forearms.
- Your ability to move your shoulders up and down.
- The movement of your shoulder blades when drawn back toward the center of your spine to keep your posture upright.

They include:

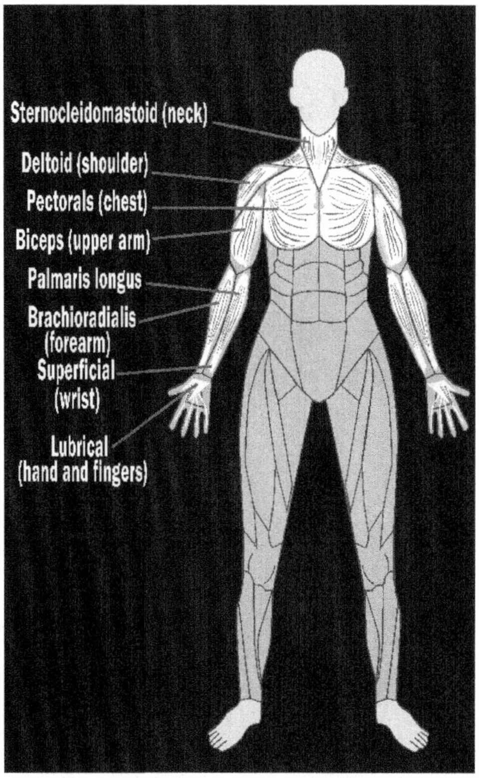

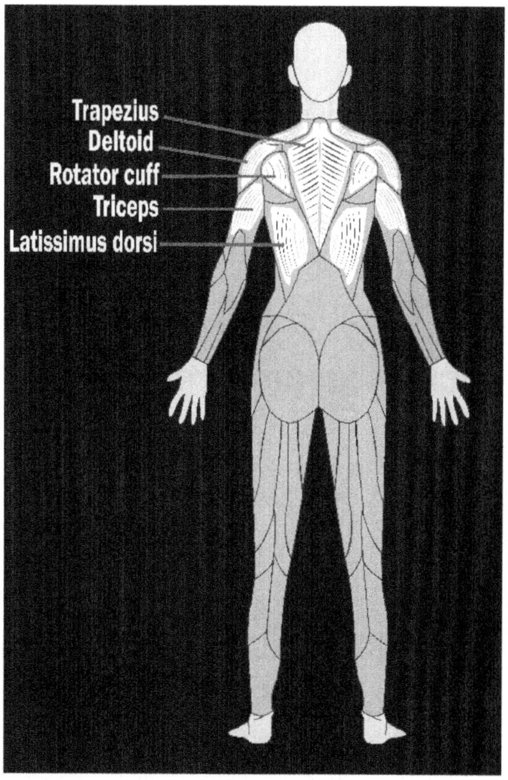

Sternocleidomastoid Muscles

The sternocleidomastoid muscles in the neck allow you to move your head forward, backward, and to each side.

Trapezius Muscles

The trapezius muscles start at the back of your head, extend across your shoulder, and down the middle of your back. These muscles play an essential role in your ability to move your shoulders and lift your arms out to the side, and they also help protect your neck and spine. You use these muscles when you shrug your shoulders or pull them back. They also play an important role in posture.

Deltoid Muscles

The deltoid muscles are the outer shoulder muscles that support your arms when you extend them in front of you, move them to the side, and reach backward. You use these muscles for activities such as hanging clothes on a line, carrying a bag of groceries, washing your hair, reaching back to scratch your back, and in sports such as swimming or tennis.

Rotator Cuff

The rotator cuff is a group of muscles and tendons that hold the shoulder joint in place and allow you to move your arm and shoulder.

Latissimus Dorsi

The latissimus dorsi is a primary back muscle stretching to the sides and behind the arms. It helps you do things like push-ups, swimming, and even breathing.

Chest or Pectoral Muscles

These muscles support the movement of your arm across or away from your body. You use these muscles when you lift a small child, move a piece of household furniture, reach far into a cupboard to retrieve an object, or get up off the floor.

Biceps and Triceps

The biceps are the significant muscles in the front of your upper arm. The triceps are the significant muscles in the back of your upper arm. These muscles allow you to bend or flex your elbow and rotate the palms of your hands upward. They enable you to hold a glass of water or turn a doorknob.

Forearm

The primary muscles in the forearm are the palmaris longus, the part of the forearm closest to your body, and the brachioradialis, which runs long outside the forearm. Your forearm provides strength to your grip so you can open a glass jar of jam or lift a suitcase onto the scale at the airport. Forearm muscles also grip a golf iron, racquet, or ball.

Wrist

The superficial muscles are in the wrist area. They play an essential role in connecting your arm to your hand. Your wrist lifts the hand to a working position. It stabilizes your forearm for writing and completing daily routine tasks.

Hands and Fingers

The lumbrical muscles are in the hands and fingers. The hand performs fine movements of the fingers and thumb to operate small tools and keyboards, allowing you to write, text using a mobile phone, paint, and play musical instruments.

Your Core Muscles

Your core muscles are those found in your torso and include the muscles in your diaphragm, abdominals, lower back, glutes, hips, and pelvic floor. A strong core is essential for supporting your spine and helping you stand up straight, maintain your balance, and remain mobile. They enable you to do most everyday household tasks because they provide the foundation for moving the arms and legs.

The primary muscles in the core include:

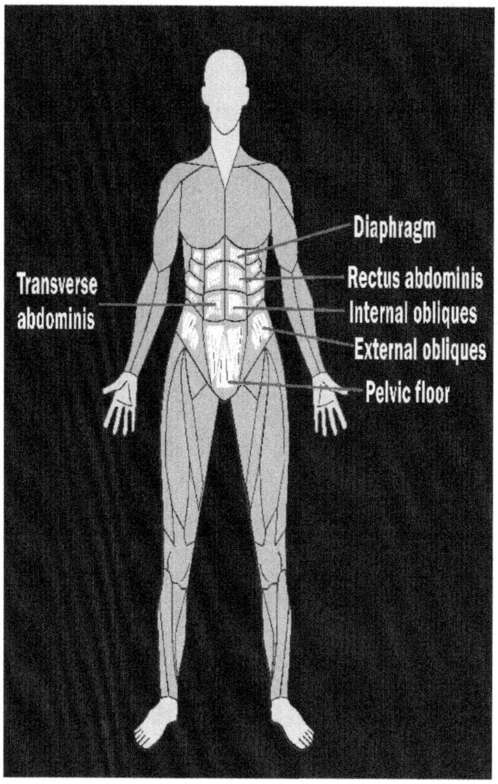

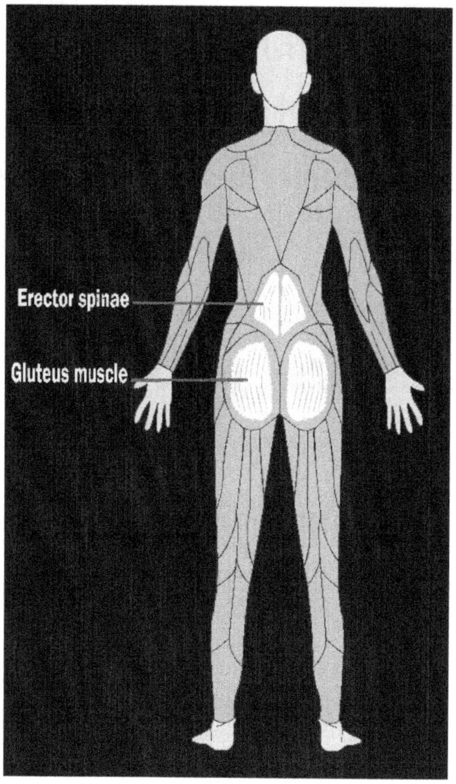

The Diaphragm

This sizeable dome-shaped muscle separates the abdomen from the chest and helps with breathing. When you breathe in, it contracts and flattens, and your abdominal muscles expand. When you breathe out, it expands, and your abdominal muscles contract, pushing air out of your lungs.

A weak diaphragm muscle can cause hernias, acid reflux, heartburn, shortness of breath, difficulty breathing when lying down, chest and upper back pains, trouble swallowing, and recurring hiccups.

Pelvic Floor Muscles

The many layers of the pelvic floor stretch like a hammock, from the pubic bone in the front to the coccyx or tailbone in the back. These muscles are used when we urinate, have a bowel movement, and delay emptying until convenient. They are also used for erectile function and ejaculation in men and voluntary contractions to assist in arousal in women. As we age, the muscles weaken due to menopause for women, straining on the toilet, heavy coughing, prostate surgery, and so on. Weakening of these muscles can lead to accidental leakage, reduced sensation in the vagina, pelvic organ prolapses, constipation, lower back pain, hip pain, and painful sex.

Transverse Abdominal Muscles (part of the abdominal muscles)

These muscles go around your waist like a corset to keep your organs in place and support your spine. They help with breathing, laughing, sneezing, and picking up the grandchildren's toys. Strengthening these muscles can also tighten your waist and help you lose unwanted inches on the waistline.

External Obliques and Internal Obliques Muscles (part of the abdominal muscles)

These muscles run from the ribcage to the hips, allowing you to bend sideways and rotate. They support your spine when you lift a heavy object, turn to look behind your shoulder, or chop wood.

Rectus Abdominis Muscles (part of the abdominal muscles)

Most know these as the “6-pack.” They extend from the top of the ribs to the pubic bone, helping you to bend your spine and tilt your pelvis. They are used to get out of bed or turn to check out something in your trouser pocket.

The Lower Back Muscles

The erector spinae, which runs from the sacrum to the upper back, is the most significant muscle in the lower back. This muscle helps hold up the spine and the glute muscles. Approximately 94% of the US population has had back pain at some point. Unless you are part of the lucky 6%, you will understand how important it is to keep your back strong. Strong back muscles are essential as they help us with most of our everyday tasks.

The Glutes and Hips Muscles

This group of muscles, consisting of around 20 different muscles, is responsible for enabling you to rotate your hips. They support your hip and allow you to move your leg in different directions, such as forward, backward, out to the side, and back inward. They also allow you to point your toes inward and outward and move your straightened leg toward your toes. The most significant muscle in this group, the gluteus maximus, is in the buttock area and helps to extend the hip and prevent falls. It allows you to take your leg back and rotate it. The smaller muscles, gluteus medius and gluteus minimus will enable you to turn your foot and move your legs to the sides while stabilizing the hip joint and helping keep your pelvis level when standing or walking on one leg. Having strong glutes can result in better balance and a stronger body.

Your Lower Body Muscles

Your lower body muscles are the strong muscles in your upper legs, lower legs, and feet. They support you when standing, walking, and moving your legs. Daily activities such as walking, climbing stairs, or standing up from a seated position become more difficult without solid leg muscles.

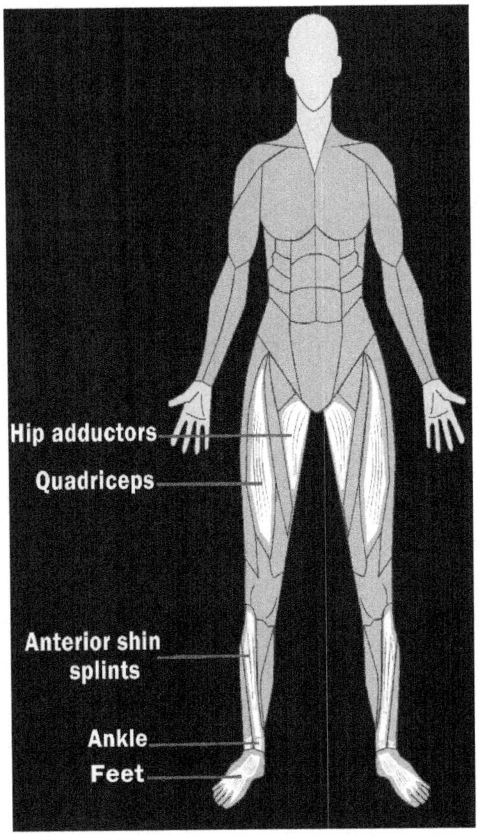

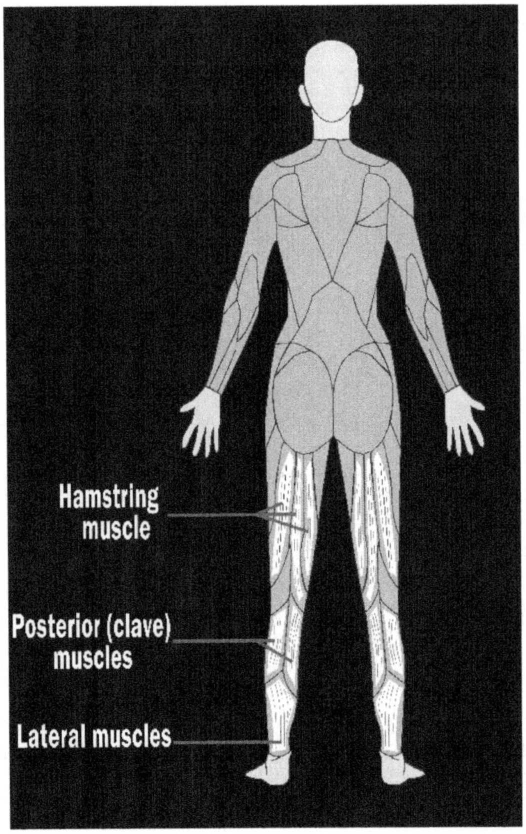

Hamstring, Quadriceps and Hip Adductor Muscles (Thigh Muscles)

The muscles in your upper leg, or thigh, comprise three strong groups. These include the hamstring muscles in the back of the thigh, the quadriceps (quads) muscles in the front of the thigh, and the hip adductor muscles on the inside of the thigh.

The hamstrings, quads, and hip adductor muscles work together to allow you to straighten and bend your leg. Together, these muscles support the knee; if they are strong, they will lessen the stress on your knee joint, reduce strain, and prevent pain. Weak muscles in your thighs often cause knee pain.

Anterior Muscles

The anterior muscles are in the front of your lower leg and support your shins. These muscles help you lift and lower your foot and extend your toes.

Posterior Muscles

The posterior muscles, including your calf muscle, run along the back of your lower leg. These muscles allow you to flex and point your toes, lock and unlock your knee, maintain good posture, and stand up straight by supporting the arch of your foot.

Lateral Muscles

The lateral muscles run outside your lower leg and stabilize your foot when walking. They also allow you to move your foot from side to side.

Ankle and Foot Muscles

There are 29 muscles in each ankle and foot. These support your weight, help you move, adapt to balance, and stabilize you. They must be strong enough to adapt to changes on the walking surface quickly. Strong muscles in the ankle lessen our risk of falling. Toes are essential in supporting the foot arch and maintaining good balance. Exercising our toes and feet is often overlooked, resulting in bunions and flat feet.

CHAPTER 5

HOW TO TAILOR YOUR EXERCISE PROGRAM TO YOU

Before we talk about tailoring your exercise program, let's quickly self-assess your current fitness level. Without being overly critical or overly optimistic, ask yourself the following questions:

- Am I easily managing my daily activities that involve lifting or carrying?
- Am I stiff all the time? Can I get up and down from a chair, do household chores, or get in and out of a car without feeling stiffness or pain?
- Can I get through the day with adequate energy, or do I constantly need to rest and take a break?
- Can I retain my balance without holding onto something as I walk or climb stairs?

- Have I fallen recently?
- Do I need to improve all four areas of my overall fitness?

This assessment is a quick way to evaluate what you initially want to focus on – building strength, increasing flexibility, improving balance, increasing endurance, or all four. If your objective is to strengthen all areas, you may want to start with the "Four Week Ageless Agility" program described in Chapter 14. This program provides weekly plans perfectly combining strength-building, flexibility, balance, and endurance exercises. You simply perform the exercises defined for each day.

Based on your answers, you may prefer the "Create Your Own" program, also discussed in Chapter 14. If you are having balance issues, you may want to focus on the balance exercises first. If you have trouble carrying groceries in from the car, you may want to start with strength-building exercises. If you wake up stiff or become stiff after you sit for any length of time, focusing on flexibility exercises may be the best for you. If you have trouble getting through the day without a nap, consider starting with endurance-building activities.

Know Your Body

It is essential to understand and acknowledge where you are in terms of physical capacity before starting this or any exercise program. If you are already in great shape, that's wonderful. Jump in where you feel comfortable and continue to improve your fitness levels.

If it has been a while since you have exercised, or you know you are out of shape. Start slowly. Give your body time to adjust to a new level of activity. You want slow, consistent improvements.

You are not in a race.

It is important to consider any underlying health conditions you have, as you may need to make some adjustments to tailor your program. For example, I have an autoimmune disease that has affected the muscles in my legs. So, for me, exercise is a delicate balance between doing too much, which can cause the illness to flare up, and doing too little, which can impact my success at building leg strength.

Are you recovering from an injury or an illness? You may need to initially reduce the amount you do or what exercises you do.

Listen to your body. You are the only one who knows how you feel; therefore, you are the best judge of what you can do.

Overweight

Exercising to lose weight and improve health is generally a good idea because of the many benefits; however, there may be some risks for those who are very overweight. These are some of the risks that you may be more prone to:

Cardiac Issues

Doctors often recommend exercise because it can help lower blood pressure by improving blood flow. If you are overweight, however, vigorous exercise may not be wise as it can cause a sudden spike in your blood pressure, which can be a health risk in people who are seriously overweight. Initially, focus more on strengthening and flexibility exercises, taking it slowly. You can gradually increase the pace when you see some benefit in weight loss. Remember to stop if you have shortness of breath or pain.

Respiratory Issues

Shortness of breath can be a reality, even after slight exertion, because the chest wall is heavier, making it harder for the lungs to expand. Initially, you can do short periods of exercise, building up as you improve. Remember to stop if you are short of breath or an oximeter shows a drop in oxygen level.

Joint Issues

If you are seriously overweight, avoid high-impact exercise. These are exercises where you are jumping or skipping and jogging. Instead, walk, swim, or cycle to avoid impact on the joints and prevent injury. Start with resistance or strength-building exercises to build muscle mass to support your weight.

Heat Exhaustion

Significantly overweight people often have more difficulty regulating body temperature, making them more likely to suffer from heat exhaustion. Avoid exercising outdoors in the hottest part of the day in the heat of summer. Instead, exercise in the early morning or late afternoon.

Dehydration

Besides difficulty regulating their body temperature, heavy people sweat more and are at higher risk of dehydration. Ensure you drink plenty of water before, during, and after exercising.

Arthritis

Approximately 80% of people over 55 are affected by arthritis, with women being more affected than men. Some estimates show that almost half the population suffers from the aches and pains of this condition. "Arthritis" refers to inflammation or swelling in one or more joints.

There is a range of diseases that fall under the same umbrella. They range from rheumatoid arthritis, gout, lupus, fibromyalgia, psoriatic arthritis, and other autoimmune disorders to osteoarthritis, a degenerative form of arthritis. Osteoarthritis, more about "wear and tear," is the most common form of arthritis, affecting over 32.5 million US adults. It is primarily found in the hands, hips, and knees. It causes pain, stiffness, and swelling, making everyday tasks difficult. In some cases, it can also result in disability due to deformity of the joints.

Physical activity is a simple, effective, drug-free way to delay the onset of arthritis. If you already have arthritis, it can help relieve and manage the pain. The only caution is to focus on low-impact exercise and to be gentle on your joints. Walking, cycling, and swimming are excellent forms of cardio exercise. Add strength-building, balance, flexibility, and other gentle endurance exercises to your regular exercise program for the best results. If you already have arthritis and have not exercised in the past, you may initially experience some pain and stiffness when you start; this will subside after your body gets used to the new activity level. Depending on your level of progress, it could take 6 to 8 weeks for your joints to get used to your new activity level, but sticking with your program will result in long-term pain relief.

Start slowly and gently. If you experience initial discomfort, modify your exercise program by exercising only a few times a week or for shorter periods each session. You can also try different exercises that focus more on strengthening the muscles, putting less pressure on your joints. Include warm-up and cool-down exercises before and after the workout. Adjust the intensity of your exercise according to your pain levels on the day.

Choose flat surfaces to prevent jarring on the knee joints, hip, and ankles when walking. Avoid taking excess pain medication before exercise, which can result in overexercising because it will mask the pain. It is better to feel what your body tells you and manage the length and intensity of exercise than to hide an injury.

Osteoporosis or Osteopenia

If you have been diagnosed with osteoporosis or osteopenia, you have some bone loss. You may be at a greater risk of breaking or fracturing a bone if you fall.

A CDC survey reports that 1 in 4 women in the United States has osteoporosis. Approximately half, or 48%, of seniors have osteopenia. Of this number, more women (52%) than men (44%) have osteopenia. The most alarming aspect of these two diseases is that there are often no symptoms until it is too late, and you break or fracture a bone.

What is osteopenia?

If you have been diagnosed with Osteopenia, your bone density levels have declined but are not yet at a level low enough to put you at a high risk of breaks and fractures.

If you have Osteopenia, your body is sending you a warning signal. It would be best if you did what you could now to slow or stop the decline and slowly start rebuilding some bone mass. Exercise can help you do this.

What is osteoporosis?

This bone disease affects people of all ages. A deficiency in calcium, magnesium, vitamin D, and other essential bone minerals causes it. Normal, healthy bones have small spaces in them. As we age, our body becomes less able to absorb and retain the necessary nutrients. These spaces become more significant, making the bones fragile.

When we are younger, there is a process of continual renewal, but in older people, especially those prone to osteoporosis, the bones break down faster than they can be renewed. They become less dense, more porous, and more prone to breaking. Women are affected the most due to decreasing estrogen levels after menopause. However, men can also develop osteoporosis due to chronic illnesses.

It would be better to start your exercise program before you begin to experience bone loss. If you already have osteoporosis, you must do what you can to stop or slow the decline; however, you must be very careful with your exercises. Doing the wrong type of exercise could result in a fracture or broken bone.

If you have osteoporosis:

Avoid all high-impact exercises such as skipping, jumping, running, or jogging, or any kind of activity that includes sudden jerky or rapid movements.

Avoid exercises that include:

- Bending forward, such as toe touches or sit-ups.
- Bending at your waist or folding forward to round out your back.
- Activities that require bending to the side.
- Exercise that requires you to form a pretzel-type position. Bending and twisting positions done together are not good.
- Jumping exercises, such as jumping jacks or jumping rope. Also, avoid jumping off a porch or truck bed.
- Exercises that involve running. Speed walking is a better alternative.
- Sports activities with a high risk of falling, such as skiing, ice skating, and rollerblading.
- Recreational activities, such as snowmobiling, riding roller coasters, horseback riding, etc., as these activities jolt your back.

Diabetes

Exercise is of utmost importance for diabetic seniors due to its broad benefits. One key advantage is its ability to control blood sugar levels effectively.

When we engage in physical activity, our muscles use glucose for energy, decreasing our blood sugar levels. For those with diabetes, exercise can help with weight loss, regulate blood lipid levels, improve blood pressure, and enhance blood sugar control.

Choosing the Right Type of Exercise

If you have diabetes, choose suitable exercise types and take additional precautions. Monitoring blood sugar levels, staying hydrated, and listening to the body's signals are vital to safe and effective exercise sessions.

It is best to avoid:

High-impact Activities

Exercises involving repetitive high-impact movements, such as running, jumping, or intense aerobic activities, can stress the joints and increase the risk of joint injuries.

If you have joint problems or complications such as neuropathy, consider low-impact alternatives like swimming, cycling, or walking.

Heavy Weightlifting

While strength training is beneficial, heavy weightlifting exercises that involve maximal or near-maximal lifts may cause a sudden increase in blood pressure.

Opt for moderate-intensity strength training with lighter weights and higher repetitions to reduce the risk of injury and excessive strain.

Exercises with a High Fall Risk

Activities with a high risk of falls or loss of balance should be avoided or approached cautiously; this includes high-intensity sports, martial arts, or activities performed at heights. Falls can lead to serious injuries, particularly for individuals with diabetes who may have compromised sensation or balance. Choose exercises that improve balance, coordination, and stability.

Exercise in Extreme Weather Conditions

Exercising in extreme temperatures, whether hot or cold, can impact blood sugar control and increase the risk of dehydration or other complications.

If you are diabetic, avoid exercising in extreme weather conditions and opt for indoor activities or exercise during cooler times of the day to maintain comfort and safety.

Exercises that Cause Excessive Strain on the Feet

Avoid exercises that strain the feet, such as high-impact jumping or repetitive foot-pounding exercises. Protecting the feet from injury or wounds due to compromised circulation or neuropathy is essential. Choose gentle exercises on the feet, such as swimming, stationary cycling, or seated exercises.

Precautions to Consider

If you are a type 1 and type 2 diabetic, you should take certain precautions to ensure safe and effective physical activity.

Here are some important considerations:

Blood Sugar Monitoring

It is essential to regularly monitor your blood sugar levels before, during, and after exercise; this helps prevent hypoglycemia (low blood sugar) or hyperglycemia (high blood sugar) during and after physical activity.

Carbohydrate Intake

Consuming a balanced meal or snack containing carbohydrates before exercise is essential, especially if blood sugar levels are below the target range. Eating a carbohydrate before exercise helps prevent hypoglycemia during the activity.

Insulin Adjustments

Adjusting to insulin dosages may be necessary depending on the intensity and duration of the exercise. Consult a healthcare professional to determine the appropriate insulin adjustments to ensure blood sugar stability during exercise.

Stay Hydrated

Hydration is crucial for type 1 and 2 diabetic seniors during exercise. Drink water before, during, and after physical activity to maintain proper hydration.

Be Prepared

Carry a source of fast-acting carbohydrates, such as glucose tablets or juice, during exercise to treat episodes of hypoglycemia.

Additionally, it is important to wear a medical identification bracelet or necklace that indicates the individual has diabetes.

Gradual Progression

Start with low-impact activities and gradually increase the duration and intensity of exercise to allow the body to adapt to the increased physical demands and reduce the risk of injuries or drastic blood sugar fluctuations.

Proper Footwear

Wear comfortable, supportive footwear to reduce the risk of foot injuries and complications. If you are diabetic, inspect your feet regularly for signs of blisters, sores, or other abnormalities.

Recognize Warning Signs

Be aware of symptoms such as dizziness, shortness of breath, chest pain, or unusual fatigue during exercise. If any of these symptoms occur, stop exercising and seek medical attention if necessary.

CHAPTER 6

ALWAYS PUT SAFETY FIRST

I hope you are excited about beginning your new exercise program and the changes it can bring to your physical well-being. I am excited for you! Just one word of caution before you start: safety must be a priority. Safety is even more critical for a senior, especially if there are balance issues or other physical conditions such as heart or breathing issues, arthritis, or a chronic physical condition. I'm sure you also know of or have heard of someone who hurt themselves by tackling a new exercise program too vigorously. Let's not join the statistics but adopt the motto, "Safety first."

Safety Considerations

Here are some safety considerations. Many of these may seem like "common sense," but it is often easy to forget them. We want to be safe. So, let's review these and make them a part of our exercise sessions.

Your Environment

Choose your exercise environment carefully before starting. It is easy to trip over the tiniest of obstacles. If you exercise indoors, inspect the floor or carpet and ensure there are no loose threads or uneven tiles. Any rough surface will increase your risk of tripping and falling. Clear the area of any items lying about. If the space is not well-lit, then switch on the light. If you have balance issues, have a sturdy chair, countertop, or a piece of heavy furniture close by so that you have support should you need it.

If you exercise outdoors, consider the route and be sure it is safe. If there is some rough terrain, it is better to go around it than go through it and increase your risk of falling. A designated pathway or pavement is a better option. If you are going to walk in a secluded place, it is always good to have a friend with you. Take a cane or walking stick if you are in a weakened condition when you start your activity. You will be able to leave that behind as you get stronger.

Don't Be Alone or without a Phone

Even if you have exercised for a while, it is best to have someone nearby to hear you if you call out.

Alternatively, whether indoors or outdoors, have your phone nearby so that you can call someone if you suddenly feel unwell or need help.

Dress for the Occasion

Exercise causes friction, and tight clothing with rough seams or fabric could restrict movement and irritate the skin. Take a few minutes to change into comfortable and slightly stretchy clothes. You don't need to go out and buy expensive gym clothes; choose stretchy or loose-fitting clothes such as T-shirts, sweatpants, or shorts.

You will need a good pair of exercise shoes, especially for walking. Ensure that your shoes are balanced, lightweight, and comfortable and that the laces are securely tied.

Stay Hydrated

Drink some water before you exercise, during your exercise, and after your workout. Even if you don't feel thirsty, your body may be hydrated. Remember, exercise will raise your body temperature, and breathing quicker and perspiring will rid your body of fluid. Stay hydrated by always having a bottle of water nearby.

Listen to Your Body

Never push through the pain. The adage "no pain, no gain" does not apply here. Initially, you may feel slight discomfort as your muscles wake up but, listen to your body. If you feel pain, stop immediately. Check the instructions to make sure that you are doing the exercise correctly.

Review the "caution" section included with most exercises for suggestions for a less strenuous variation.

Slow and consistent movements are best. Simply reducing the number of repetitions may be all you need to do. Or take a short break. Initially, there may be a minor soreness after an exercise session as muscles work again, but you should not feel severe achiness or sharp pain.

The bottom line is: If you feel pain, stop, adjust, and try again. If you still feel pain, skip the exercise and try again later.

Take It Slow and Steady

You are not in a competition. Set your own goal and your own pace. Go slowly and steadily to strengthen, improve your balance, and regain flexibility. Consistency is what will bring you the reward. Pushing yourself beyond your level will result in injury and overload on your body, which will set you back rather than bring success.

Include Warm-Up/Cool-Down Exercises

Play it safe and start your exercise program with low-intensity warm-up exercises. Like a car's engine, our bodies work better when they get a chance to warm up. Would you consider driving your vehicle on a cold winter morning without giving it a little time to warm up? Give your body the same consideration. Cells work better when they get oxygen, and warming up allows the blood to begin to circulate and transport it to each cell. Only about 20% of the blood volume is in muscles at rest, and you want about 80% to be there when you exercise, so warming up gives it a little time to get there. As you begin slowly, your core body temperature will rise, and your muscles will become more supple, which means less chance of injury.

Sudden vigorous exercise can also stress the heart and lungs. Warm-up exercises prepare the body by slowly increasing the circulation and heart rate. If you have a heart condition, arthritis, or other health issues, you may need more time to loosen up your muscles so the joints will lubricate, and the muscles will wake up.

Dynamic exercises get the body moving, one of the best ways to warm up. They will put your joints and muscles through a full range of motion, ensuring you lubricate them and do not strain anything. Chapter 11 provides more detail on dynamic exercises.

Talk to Your Doctor

The exercises in this book are low-impact and designed to be safe and gentle. However, if you have one of the health issues discussed earlier or any other medical or physical issue, please safeguard yourself by consulting with your physician before starting this or any other exercise program.

CHAPTER 7

WHAT ABOUT EQUIPMENT?

Some of the exercises in this book recommend the use of inexpensive equipment.

You do not need aids to do these exercises, but using equipment can be beneficial. Using equipment can:

- Help to control the path of the movement you are making.
- Match the force of your muscle strength, so you will get double the benefit with half the effort.
- Make it easier to develop the correct form; using the proper form reduces the risk of injury.
- Help you monitor your progress as you increase the weight of the equipment or resistance.
- More easily increase muscle strength.

Most recommended items are low-cost and easily purchased online or at your local sports store. You can substitute the equipment with items customarily found around the house if you have a tight budget. The key takeaway is that you do not need to purchase anything to start this exercise program. Just start with what you have.

Equipment used in some of the exercises in this book includes:

A Sturdy Chair

A sturdy chair is the only aid that is not optional. Many exercises in this book are seated or use a chair for support and balance. You will need a sturdy chair that will not wobble as you work out. Avoid using a chair on rollers that will move as you move while exercising. Although some chairs have a braking mechanism, these are also not recommended as the exercise movement will weaken the braking mechanism, and it could suddenly give way. Ensure the chair is fixed and cannot slide on the floor surface while exercising. You may find it easier to do some exercises using a chair with arms, a chair without arms, or a stool. Use the chair type that is most comfortable for you.

Light Weights

Dumbells

Dumbbells are used for some exercises as they will help you build strength. They are recommended but optional. If you decide to purchase a set of dumbbells, be sure to consider these guidelines:

How to Select Your Dumbbells:

Determining the proper dumbbell weight for an older person differs for each person. If you haven't exercised in a while, are recovering from a physical impairment, or have arthritis, start with a lightweight dumbbell. If you are healthy and active and have been exercising for a while, you should be able to start with a heavier weight. The important point is the weight you select should be heavy enough to challenge you without causing injury.

Start by selecting a moderately heavy dumbbell that you can lift 10–15 times without too much strain (where lifting means holding the weights at your side and bringing them to your chest). Start with a 1-lb or 2-lb weight and increase it until you are comfortable with the chosen weight.

If you are unsure, start with the lower-pound weight. Some dumbbells are coated with a nonslip silicon covering and are comfortable. If your weights are metal and you find this hard on your hands, get a pair of nonslip gym gloves with cut-off fingers for a comfortable grip. The added advantage to using these is warmth if you exercise outdoors in colder weather.

For low-budget alternatives, fill a soda or water bottle with water and freeze it. Remember to use the frozen bottle with a towel or cloth wrapped around it to prevent freezer burn on your hands. A can of vegetables in each hand will also work for weight training.

Ankle Weights

Ankle weights are small weights inserted into an elastic or Velcro-type band that wraps around the ankle. The products with a Velcro band are best as they allow you to adjust the fit easily. As with dumbbells, selecting the correct weight for ankle weights is also important.

How to Select Your Ankle Weights

Start with a low weight around your ankle. Sit back in a chair and lift your leg out straight. Select a starting weight that allows you to raise your leg 10–15 times without discomfort. Some ankle weights will allow you to insert weights from 1 pound to 5 pounds in order to increase the weight over time.

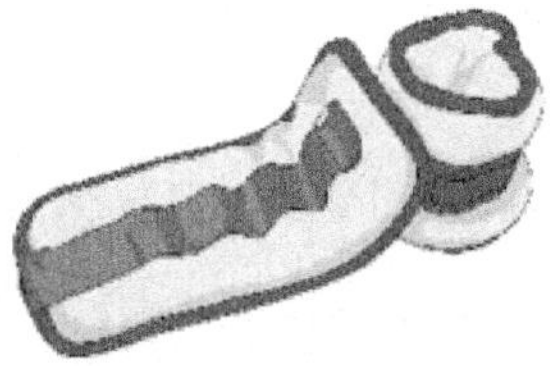

You can use a bag of sugar, flour, or any other item from your kitchen cupboard for a low-budget alternative. Just attach it to your ankle with a headband or insert it into socks.

Small Balls

Small Exercise Ball

Some exercises include using a softly inflated, 6–9-inch diameter ball. A small child's ball will also work. If you are on a budget, use a folded or rolled towel instead of a ball.

Tennis Ball

You can use a tennis ball for some exercises. It is also helpful for "rolling out" muscle spasms if you position the ball between the wall and the sore muscle and roll it around. For a low-budget alternative, use a small child's ball or string or yarn rolled into a ball.

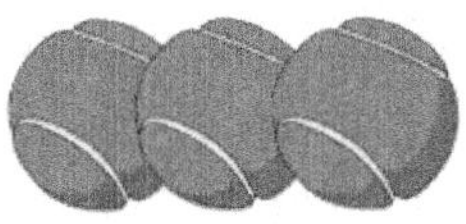

Other Items

Small Hand Towel

Some of the exercises recommend using a folded towel or towels as an aid to provide additional leverage when doing the exercise.

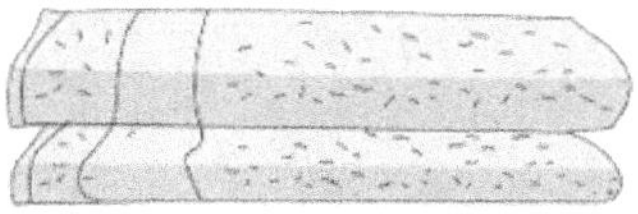

Yoga Style Mat

Some of the exercises are done lying down. You can do these on your bed, or if you can easily get down and then up again, you can do them on the floor. If you do these on the floor, you may find it better to use a nonslip yoga mat; this will also provide some cushioning to make exercising more comfortable. For a low-cost alternative, use a large bath towel or folded blanket; just be sure it doesn't slip on the flooring.

CHAPTER 8

IT'S YOUR CHOICE

Thus far, we have discussed what happens to our bodies as we age. We have debunked the common myths that can keep us from exercising. We have reviewed the four types of exercises seniors need: strength-building, flexibility, balance, and endurance. We have looked at how to tailor your exercise program to consider any physically limiting challenges you may have.

In Part II of this book, we will review each exercise type and provide numerous exercises for each. We will discuss flexible exercise plans you can create to meet your unique needs or follow the "Four Week Ageless Agility" program. We will also introduce "Fit Fun" exercises that you can easily fit into your daily activities.

But before we go any further, let's pause for a moment to think about the following two questions:

- Are you ready to commit to improving your health?
- Are you ready to commit to an exercise program?

If your answer is a resounding YES, fantastic! Then, move on to the next section.

If your answer is a definite NO, then there is no need to continue reading this book. I sincerely wish you the very best as you move through this special time in your life.

If you are unsure, let's discuss why you may be hesitating. Perhaps you understand the benefits and drawbacks of not exercising but have concerns about your ability to do this. There may be another reason. Whatever the reason, I encourage you to think about why you purchased this book in the first place. What fitness issues are you experiencing now or want to prevent experiencing as you age? What are the probable consequences if these are not addressed? For most of us to make a significant change in our lives, we need a good reason. We need to know what that reason is, and it needs to be substantial enough to get us out of the recliner.

We also need to understand what is holding us back and address these concerns and fears. So, if you are still hesitant, I encourage you to continue reading this book; you may resolve your areas of concern. If not, commit to talking with your doctor about the right program. The most important thing is for you to move forward.

How Do You Stay Motivated?

You have decided you want a healthier future! I am excited for you! Now, let's discuss that concern lurking in your mind: How do I stick to it? Most of us have enthusiastically started a new diet or exercise program, only to see our excitement wane as life interferes with our good intentions. So, how do we stay committed and motivated? Here are some tips:

Schedule a Time for Exercise Every Day

If exercise is not in your schedule, it is very easy to skip it. It is important to give your exercise schedule the same level of importance as you most likely give your medication schedule. If you take medication, you usually have a specific time each day when you take it; this is most likely a high priority because you know it is vital to your well-being. Adopt the same attitude and commitment to your exercise program. Staying fit is as crucial to your well-being as taking the appropriate medications.

Schedule Your Exercise Time When Best for You

We are all different; some are morning people, and others peak later in the day. Scientists tell us that our body runs on a circadian rhythm clock, which causes mental and physical changes throughout the 24-hour cycle. It influences us when we feel tired or hungry or are most energetic and productive. So, choose a time of day when you are alert and the most active to exercise.

Make Exercise a Part of Your Daily Routine

In addition to your scheduled exercise time, find ways during your day to add exercise and movement to your day. Implement some of the Fit Fun exercises described later in the book. Take the stairs instead of the elevator. Do arm and leg exercises while you watch TV. Park at the far end of the parking lot so you must walk further to the store. Step away from the computer every 30 minutes to stretch or walk around for a few minutes.

Make It Fun

Focus on activities you enjoy. Put on lively, upbeat music to get you in the mood. Vary the routine frequently to keep it interesting. Try walking, dancing, swimming, or cycling. Mix it up. Try walking or cycling in an exciting environment with things to look at, like little woodland animals, plants, rolling hills, the beach, etc. Explore new pathways and trails. Try walking in the mall as you enjoy window shopping or want to avoid the hot or cold weather outside. Use a treadmill or stationary bicycle while watching your favorite TV show. Dance around the house as you do your housework or chores. The objective is to keep moving.

Exercise with a Friend or Neighbor

Exercise is always more fun with someone else. Try one of the many online platforms to exercise "with" someone." Connect with small grandchildren who can exercise in their homes while you exercise in your home in a different town. Ask your partner or a friend to exercise with you. Make it something you enjoy doing together. Instead of getting together for coffee and cakes, catch up while you exercise, and then have that coffee. Make your time together something to look forward to.

Set Goals

Start with simple, achievable goals that are realistic for your fitness level. Do not start with the most challenging exercises if you haven't exercised for years. This book includes a beginner and intermediate program with a detailed weekly plan for four weeks. This makes it easy. Your goal is to simply follow the schedule for the week. If you are a 'do-it-yourself' gal or guy, choose three to five simple exercises and start from there. Do these exercises for a few days, add more, and go from there.

It can also be helpful to break your goal into a series of mini goals that will build upon each other. Let's assume that you want to be able to walk vigorously for 30 minutes a day, four days a week, but you know this will be initially difficult for you. Perhaps you are recovering from an illness, or you are overweight, or you haven't exercised in a long time. If you try to do the full 30 minutes on day one, you will probably end up winded and overtired and find new parts of your body that now ache. You might decide that you can't do this and quit. The solution is to break down your goal into smaller, more manageable mini goals, allowing you to start without overdoing yourself and gradually build the stamina you need to accomplish your goal.

For example:

- Week 1 – Walk for 10 minutes at a moderate pace three times during the week.
- Week 2 – Walk at an increased speed for 10 minutes three times during the week.
- Week 3 – Walk at the increased pace for 15 minutes four times during the week.
- Week 4 – Walk for 20 minutes at a moderate pace four times during the week.
- Week 5 – Walk for 20 minutes at a vigorous pace four times during the week.
- Week 6 – Walk for 30 minutes at a lively pace four times during the week.

By the end of Week 6, you will have achieved your goal!

You get the picture! Set small, achievable, measurable goals and feel your confidence and physical fitness grow.

Record Progress

Make a note in your diary each time you exercise. Record the time, the pace, and the activity; this will let you see the progress and know how you are doing. You can adjust your timeline if you must but try to keep your goals ahead of what you can achieve. Seeing your progress in black and white will be motivating as it reminds you of your achievements.

Give Yourself a Reward

Pat yourself on the back when you achieve an exercise goal. Allow yourself to feel good about it. Reward yourself by doing something you love to do—listen to music for 30 minutes, have a bubble bath, or read a book.

When you reach a larger goal, spoil yourself with a new pair of walking shoes, a lunch out with a friend, or whatever helps to keep you motivated.

Be Adaptable

If you have an exhausting day, go easy on yourself and rest. If you get invited to a day out with family, it's okay to go and enjoy yourself. Just get back on track as soon as you can.

Stop Procrastinating

If you find yourself procrastinating because you already feel too busy, look for ways to free up time so that you can make exercise your priority for now.

Are there TV shows that you watch, but don't enjoy that much? Could this time be used for exercise? Or can you do Fit Fun exercises or ride a stationary bike while watching the TV program? Be creative and look for ways to make exercise a priority.

When All Else Fails

Have you ever set a goal to change something significant in your life, such as to lose weight, stop smoking, or, in this case, start an exercise program and get to a point when you think you want to quit? You find yourself thinking, "I don't want to do this anymore." If you reach this point and all else has failed, you must "Remember your WHY."

What is it that you love to do? What brings you immense joy and happiness? Is your lack of adequate physical capacity preventing you from doing these things? When all else fails, bringing your "WHY" into a full-screen view can keep you going; it can be the catalyst that motivates you not to quit. You may need to take a break and rest, but you will remain committed to keeping your body strong and flexible to have the physical capacity to do what you love.

Creating a vision board is a great way to keep your WHY front and center. A vision board is usually a picture or a collage of images representing your "Why." Seeing these images and photographs helps you visualize you enjoying these beautiful events or accomplishments. They can help motivate you to do the things you need to do now so that these things can become a reality in your future.

I have already shared my "Why." It is all about wanting to enjoy my family and my grandchildren. I also want to look and feel great as I age. So, I have a small area in my bedroom with pictures of my grandchildren and a picture of Universal Studios in Orlando. I plan on spending a vacation with them there soon, and I want to be physically able to walk around the park all day and enjoy the rides with them. I also have another picture of me with my older granddaughters and the Eiffel Tower in Paris. I want to take my fashion-loving granddaughters there. That will require a lot of stamina and the ability to walk a reasonable distance. I also have a photo of myself taken a few years ago when I was looking and feeling my best. These pictures help motivate me to shake off the "COVID body." As I look at these pictures daily, I can visualize myself enjoying these activities with the physical capability, strength, and flexibility I need to realize these things. They help motivate me because every time I start to feel lazy and consider skipping exercise for the day, they remind me why I don't want to do that. They remind me that these beautiful events will only happen if I can physically do them.

What will you put on your vision board? If you want to travel, cut out and paste travel brochure photos of your next destination. It could be you playing on a new golf course with your friends. It could be a dance studio with you and your significant other whirling around the dance floor. It may be doing fun activities with your grandchildren. Challenge yourself to create your vision board and start visualizing a healthier, more vital you enjoying your senior years the way you envision and desire them to be. Make this the first step to starting your new exercise program!

Sharing the Golden Age

Aging is not 'lost youth' but a new stage of opportunity and strength. – Betty Friedan

When I told you my "why" for writing this book, I told you the choice I was faced with: Accept the fact that I was going to spend my golden years confined to a chair and reliant on my family, or take action to maintain my independence, working to regain my strength, balance, and flexibility.

IT WAS A NO-BRAINER when I laid it out like that for myself. The idea of watching my grandchildren play and not being able to keep up with them, watching from the sidelines, gave me the worst feeling—and not just for me, but for everyone like me.

I have much more strength and energy now, and I continue to put the work in, so I'll never be in that situation again. As my journey has continued, I've discovered an increasing passion for helping others make the same changes.

We're lucky to have a far greater life expectancy than previous generations, but we can only experience this blessing if we're healthy enough to enjoy it. I want to help as many people as possible to maintain health, independence, and vitality well into their golden years.

You're determined to take charge of your health, or you wouldn't have gotten this far. Would you join me in my quest to spread this information further?

By leaving a review of this book on Amazon, you'll show other seniors that they can act and feel 10 to 20 years younger than their chronological age.

Simply by telling other readers how this book has helped you and what they'll find inside, you'll show them that aging doesn't have to involve a rapid decline in health and fitness.

Thank you so much for your support.

PART II

LET'S EXERCISE

CHAPTER 9

TERMINOLOGY AND NOTATIONS

Many exercises in this book utilize terms or notations commonly used in the exercise community or are unique to this book. Their explanations are provided here, rather than repeating them in each exercise.

Standard Terminology

Repetitions

Repetition refers to the number of times that you will do an exercise in the workout session. If the instructions say ten repetitions, you will do that exercise sequence ten times.

Counting Seconds

Some exercises instruct you to hold a stretch or position for a specific

number of seconds, such as 30 seconds. If you don't want to use a stopwatch, you can roughly count seconds by saying at a steady rate,
ONE (thousand),
TWO (thousand),
THREE (thousand), etc.

Sets

This term refers to the number of times you will perform the repetitions. So, if an exercise says ten repetitions, two sets, you do the exercise sequence ten times, take a few-second break, and then execute it ten more times, making up two sets.

If the exercise says, "Hold for 30 seconds", this is one set.

Stand Tall or Sit Tall

If the exercise description says, "**Stand Tall**" or "**Sit Tall**," this means you should:

- Stand up straight or sit up straight in a chair.
- Imagine that your chest is drawn up by a string attached to your sternum and lifted to about a 45-degree angle.
- Imagine your head being raised by an imaginary line attached to the crown of your head.
- Keep your shoulders back and down.

Engage Your Core

The core is the central part of your body. When these muscles are tightened and well engaged, you will be better balanced and able to stay steady and stable while exercising. If the exercise description says, "Engage Your Core," this means you should:

- Breathe in.
- Tighten the muscles along the pelvic floor and pull your stomach muscles in and up. You can imagine you are trying to pull up the zipper on a pair of trousers that are a little too tight. Start from your pubic bone and zip up toward your sternum.
- Keep this position as you breathe and perform the exercise.

Ramp Up

Many exercises include a "ramp-up" option." These are instructions for increasing the intensity of the exercise. Use this option after you have mastered the movement and are comfortable performing the total number of repetitions and sets.

Caution

There is a “caution” section for most exercises. The “caution” section will give you instructions and recommendations on reducing the intensity of the movement if the exercise is too strenuous for you now.

Exercise Notations

Many exercises recommend the use or optional use of equipment such as weights, balls, towels, etc. Using the equipment item for these exercises can provide a more substantial workout and better results. If you find using the equipment difficult, start without it. The exercise will still be beneficial; you can add the equipment when you are stronger.

These exercises have been notated with one of these icons:

Weights

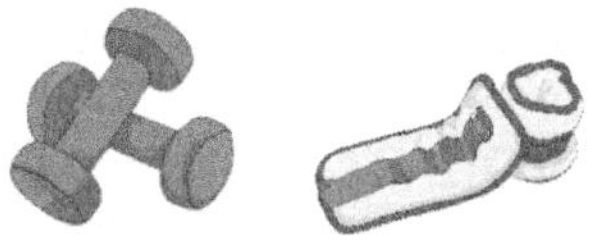

You will find these symbols notated with exercises that build strength.

Ball

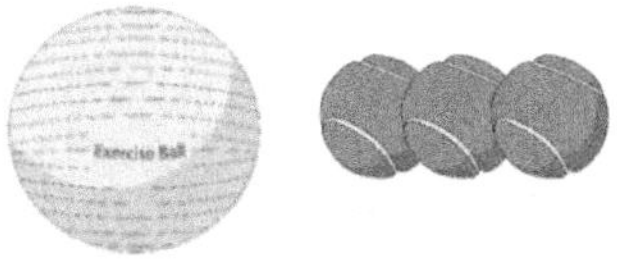

A ball symbol indicates that using a ball with the exercise will provide the best results.

Towel

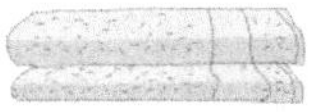

Some exercises recommend using a folded or rolled towel.

FIT FUN (Fitness Fun)

Some exercises have also been classified as "FIT FUN" exercises. Add these exercises as you go about your day. They are an easy, fun way to make fitness a part of your daily life. For example, you can do heel raises while cooking, washing dishes, or woodworking in the garage. You can do wall presses during a coffee break at work or while waiting for the cake to come out of the oven. Fit Fun exercises for your feet, hands, knees, wrists, and shoulders can be done while sitting and watching TV. You can fit as many of these exercises into your typical day as you like, and it's a fun way of making sure you move and exercise without even thinking about it.

Note that some exercises may have both the FIT FUN and weights symbols. These exercises can be done as FIT FUN exercises if you do them without weights.

Other Notes

Breathing Correctly

Breathing correctly is important when doing an exercise. Do not hold your breath; your body will perform better if it gets a constant oxygen supply. Each exercise includes breathing instructions, but generally, proper breathing is as follows.

Breathe deeply through your nose. You want the air to circulate through your lungs and belly just before doing the exercises' muscle-lengthening position. Then breathe out through your mouth when doing the exercises' muscle-shortening portion.

For example, if you are doing a modified squat that requires you to stand, sit down on the seat of the chair, and then stand again, you would breathe as follows:

- Breathe in as you stand.
- Breathe out as you squat down on the chair.
- Breathe in as you raise back up to a standing position.

This rhythm works with the exercise; when you are breathing with the rhythm, you can typically do more repetitions.

Exercise Position

The description indicates whether the exercise is done standing, seated, kneeling, or lying. If the exercise is done lying and you cannot easily get up and down from the floor, you can do these exercises on your bed.

CHAPTER 10

BUILDING STRENGTH

Strength training is the first pillar of your exercise program. The many benefits of strength training are discussed in Chapter 3.

The best way to develop muscle and strength is to Incorporate resistance into the exercise. Strength or resistance training typically includes lifting weights by machine, using free weights, or using resistance bands for body weight-bearing exercises. This type of exercise causes our muscles to contract to raise a "heavy" object against the pull of gravity. The strength-building exercises in this book use your natural body weight and dumbbells or ankle weights as the primary sources of resistance. Because this book is designed for seniors who may just be getting started or last exercised a while ago, all exercises can also be done without using weights. If this is you, begin without the weights and build up to using them as you get stronger. If you are using weights, please review the guidelines for selecting the correct weights in Chapter 7.

How often should I do strength-building exercises?

The CDC recommends that anyone over 65 participate in strength-building exercises at least twice weekly; more on this in Chapter 14.

A reminder:

Many of the exercises use standard terms and notations. For a refresher on these terms, refer to Chapter 9.

Strength Training – Upper Body

Shoulder Raises

Position: Seated

Equipment Needed: Weights

Primary Area(s) Worked: Shoulders

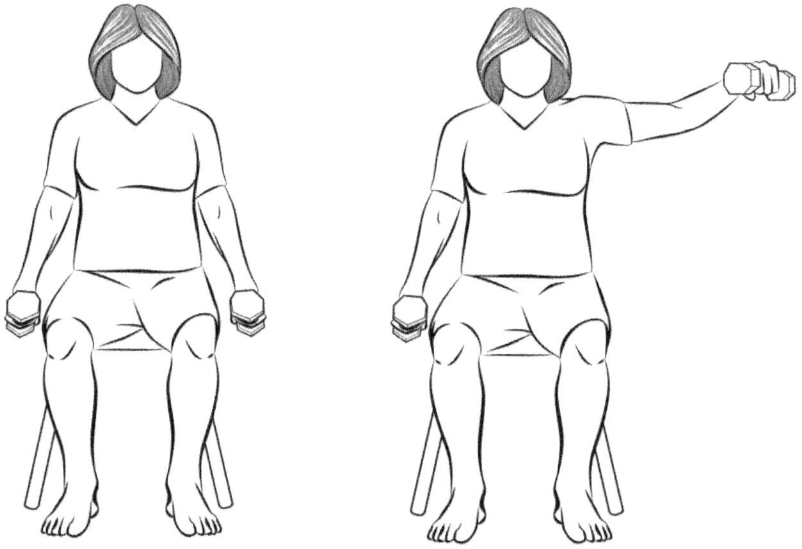

1. **Sit tall** and slightly forward in the chair. **Engage your core** throughout the exercise. Place your feet flat on the floor.
2. Hold a weight in each hand, with your palms facing down. Drop your arms to your side and slightly bend your elbow. Breathe in.
3. Using your shoulder muscle, breathe out and slowly raise your right arm out beside you to shoulder height.
4. Breathe in and gently release your arm back to the starting position.

5. Using your shoulder muscle, breathe out and slowly raise your left hand out beside you to shoulder height.
6. Breathe in and gently release it back to the starting position.
7. Start with 10 repetitions on both arms. Gradually build up to 3 sets or 30 repetitions.

Slowly ramp up:

Once you have the correct technique and feel confident, try increasing the weight. So, if you started with a 2-lb weight, do the exercises with a 3-lb weight, and so on.

Caution:

Stop immediately if this exercise causes you pain. Lift your arms as high as you can without causing pain. You should be able to slowly increase the degree of the lift as you get stronger. You can also try using a lower pound weight or doing the exercise without weights; use your clenched fists instead. If you still feel pain, skip this exercise and come back to it when you have more strength and flexibility.

Shoulder Squeeze

Position: Standing

Equipment Needed: Optional Weights

Primary Area(s) Worked: Shoulders

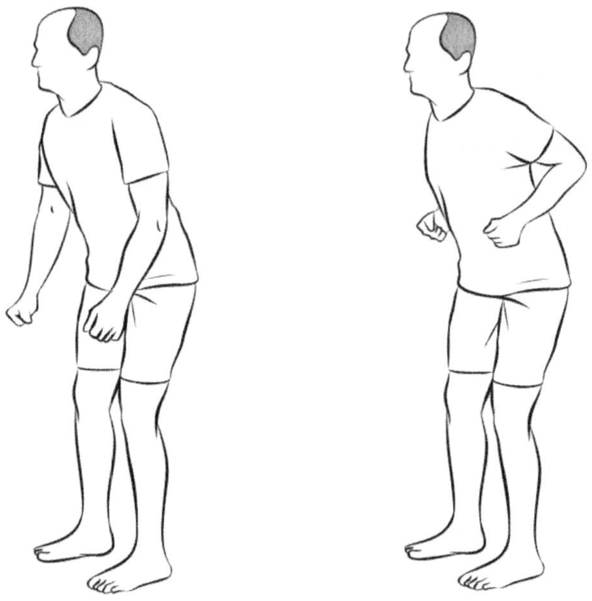

1. **Stand tall** with your shoulders back and your feet shoulder-width apart. **Engage your core** throughout the exercise.
2. Bend forward at about 90 degrees, keeping your back straight. Bring your arms slightly in front of you with elbows slightly bent. Breathe in.
3. As you breathe out, squeeze your shoulder blades together and bring your arms and elbows back and up.
4. Bring your arms back to the starting position as you breathe in. Keep your chest up.

5. Start with 10 repetitions. Gradually build up to 3 sets or 30 repetitions.

Slowly ramp up:

Once you have the correct technique and feel confident, increase the repetitions. Instead of making a fist, you can use light weights.

Caution:

Stop immediately if this exercise causes you pain. Adjust to bring your arms back as far as you can without causing pain. You should be able to slowly increase the degree of the lift as you get stronger. If you still feel pain, skip this exercise and return to it when you have more strength and flexibility.

Rotator Cuff Strengthen

Position: Seated or Standing

Equipment Needed: Weights

Primary Area(s) Worked: Shoulders, Middle Back

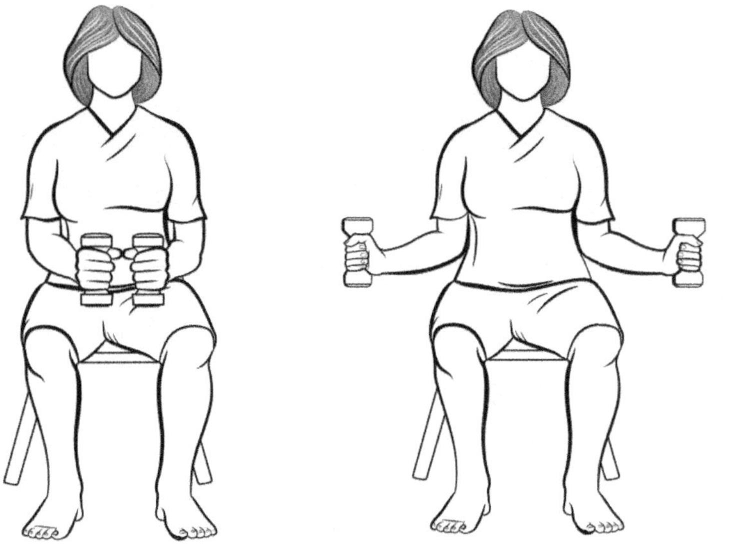

1. **Stand tall** or **sit tall** with your shoulders back and down and your spine straight. **Engage your core** throughout the exercise.
2. Hold a weight in each hand, palms facing each other. Your hands should be about 6 inches apart in the front of your body.
3. Keep your elbows close to your waist. There should be no pressure on your neck or shoulders. Breathe In.
4. Breathe out and slowly move your arms out to the sides. Squeeze your shoulder blades together as you move your arms out.
5. Breathe in and slowly bring them back to the starting position.

6. Start with 10 repetitions. Gradually build up to 3 sets or 30 repetitions.

Slowly ramp up:

Once you have the correct technique and feel confident, try increasing the weight. So, if you started with a 2-lb weight, do the exercises with a 3-lb weight, and so on.

Caution:

Stop immediately if this exercise causes you pain. Bring your arms out as far as possible without causing pain. You should be able to slowly increase the degree of the outward movement as you get stronger. You can also try using a lower pound weight or exercising without weights; use your clenched fists instead. If you still feel pain, skip this exercise and return to it when you have more strength and flexibility.

Seated Push-Back 

Position: Seated

Equipment Needed: Weights

Primary Area(s) Worked: Shoulder, Chest

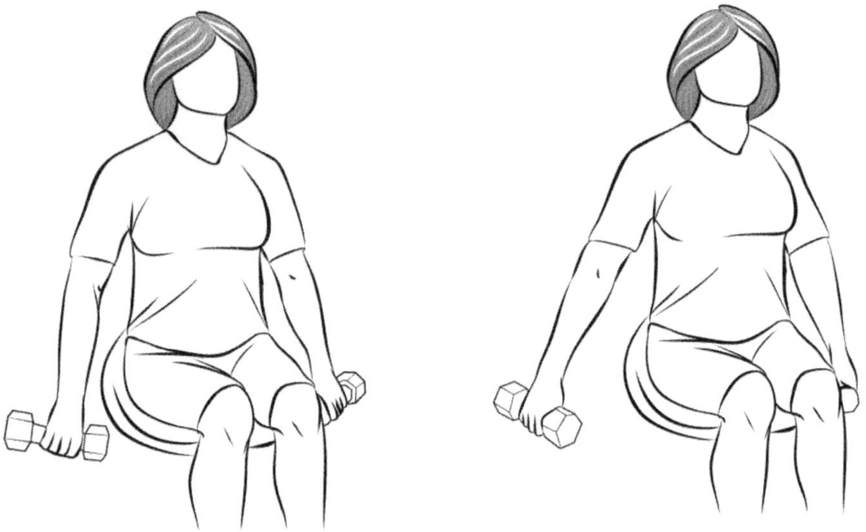

1. **Sit tall** and slightly forward in the chair. **Engage your core** throughout the exercise. Place your feet flat on the floor.
2. Hold a weight in each hand. Drop your arms to your side with your palms facing your body.
3. Tuck your chin in, push your chest out and breathe in.
4. Breathe out and slowly bring your arms back, squeezing your shoulder blades together. Open your chest as you pull your shoulders together.
5. Breathe in as you slowly move back to the starting position.

6. Start with 10 repetitions. Gradually build up to 3 sets or 30 repetitions.

Slowly ramp up:

Once you have the correct technique and feel confident, try increasing the weight. So, if you started with a 2-lb weight, do the exercises with a 3-lb weight, and so on.

Caution:

Stop immediately if this exercise causes you pain. Bring your arms back as far as possible without causing pain. You should be able to slowly increase the degree of the lift as you get stronger. You can also try using a lower pound weight or exercising without weights; use your clenched fists instead. If you still feel pain, skip this exercise and return to it when you have more strength and flexibility.

Dumbbell Row

Position: Kneeling

Equipment: Weights

Primary Area(s) Worked: Shoulders, Middle Back

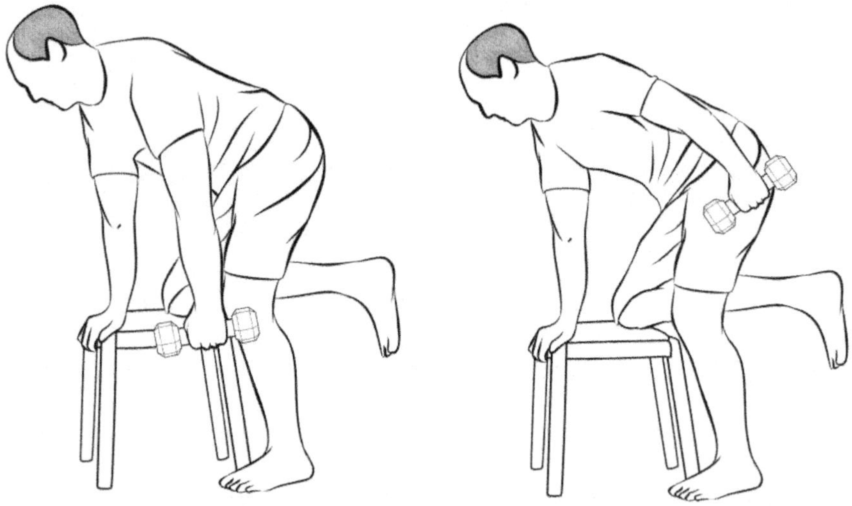

1. Begin with your right knee on a bench or chair with your right hand supporting you.
2. **Engage your core** throughout the exercise.
3. Slightly bend your right elbow to ensure no pressure on the shoulder or neck. Your back should have a slight inward curve.
4. With the weight in your left hand, bring your left hand down along your thigh. Breathe in.
5. Breathe out and gently pull your arm back along your thigh, keeping your arm close to your body. Your movement should be back and forth, not up and down.

6. Gently return your arm to the initial position along your thigh. Repeat 10 times.
7. Change positions so that your left knee and left hand are on the bench or chair, and the weight is in your right hand.
8. Repeat the exercise.
9. Start with 10 repetitions on both arms, then gradually build up to 3 sets or 30 repetitions.

Slowly ramp up:

Once you have the correct technique and feel confident, try increasing the weight. So, if you started with a 2-lb weight, do the exercises with a 3-lb weight, and so on.

Caution:

Stop immediately if this exercise causes you pain. Bring your arms as far back as you can without causing pain. You should be able to slowly increase the degree of the lift as you get stronger. You can also try using a lower pound weight or exercising without weights; use your clenched fists instead. If you still feel pain, skip this exercise and return to it when you have more strength and flexibility.

Push Back

Position: Kneeling

Equipment Needed: Weights

Primary Area(s) Worked: Shoulders, Chest, Middle Back

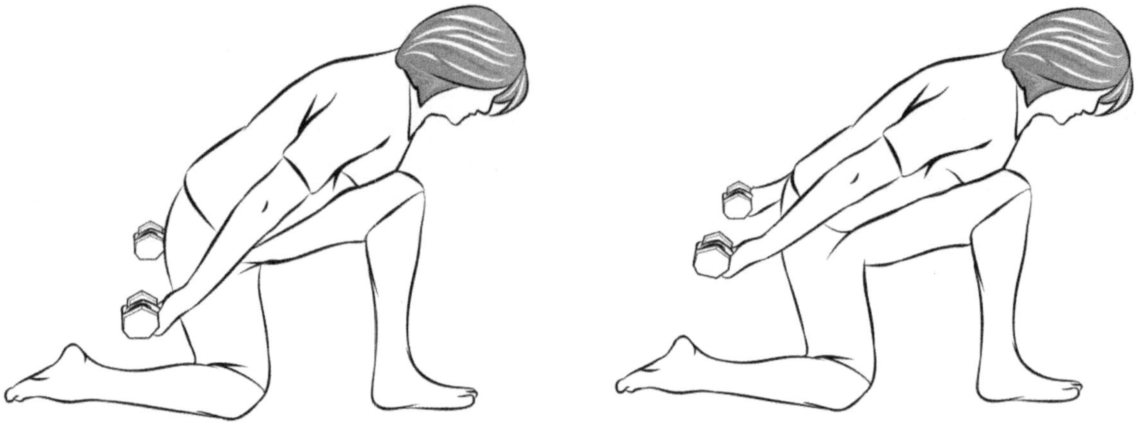

1. Begin in a kneeling position. Bring one leg forward and extend your chest over the forward thigh.
2. Place a weight in each hand.
3. Tuck your chin in, push your chest out, and slightly down. Breathe in.
4. Breathe out, press your arms back toward the ceiling, and squeeze your shoulder blades together.
5. Breathe in and move your arms back to the starting position.
6. Begin with 10 repetitions on both arms and gradually build up to 3 sets or 30 repetitions.

Slowly ramp up:

Once you have the correct technique and feel confident, try increasing the weight. So, if you started with a 2-lb weight, do the exercises with a 3-lb weight, and so on.

Caution:

Stop immediately if this exercise causes you pain. Bring your arms as far back as you can without causing pain. You should be able to slowly increase the degree of the lift as you get stronger. You can also try using a lower pound weight or exercising without weights; use your clenched fists instead. If you still feel pain, skip this exercise and return to it when you have more strength and flexibility.

Arm Lifts

Position: Seated

Equipment Needed: Weights

Primary Area(s) Worked: Upper Back, Shoulders

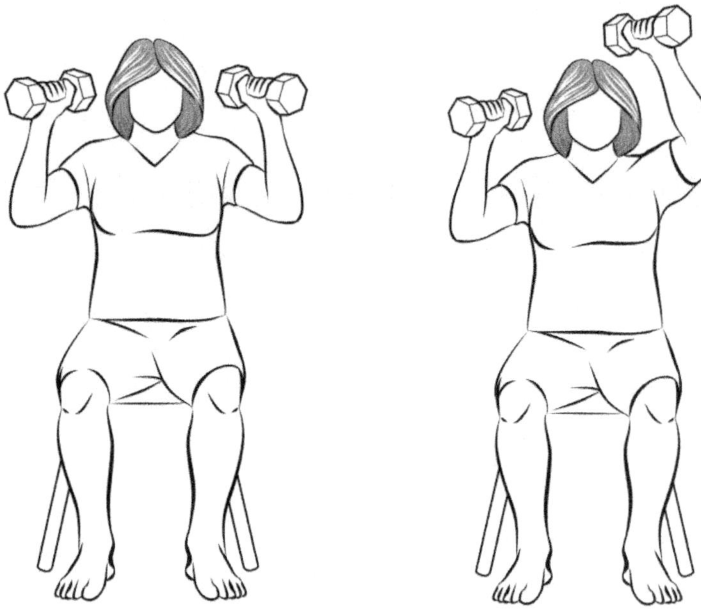

1. **Sit tall**, leaning back in the chair. **Engage your core** throughout the exercise. Your feet should be flat on the floor, your shoulders straight.
2. Hold a weight in each hand, with your palms facing each other. Bring your arms up to your shoulders. Breathe in.
3. Breathe out as you slowly lift your right arm up above your head.
4. Breathe in as you bring it back to the starting position.
5. Breathe out as you slowly lift your left arm up above your head.

6. Breathe in as you bring it back to the starting position. Start with 10 repetitions on both arms. Gradually build up to 3 sets or 30 repetitions.

Slowly ramp up:

Once you have the correct technique and you feel confident, try increasing the weight. So, if you started with a 2-lb weight, do the exercises with a 3-lb weight, and so on.

Caution:

Stop immediately if this exercise causes you pain. Lift your arms as high as you can without causing pain. You should be able to slowly increase the degree of the lift as you get stronger. You can also try using a lower pound weight or doing the exercise without weights; use your clenched fists instead. If you still feel pain, skip this exercise and come back to it when you have more strength and flexibility.

Chest Extension

Position: Seated

Equipment Needed: Weights

Primary Area(s) Worked: Chest

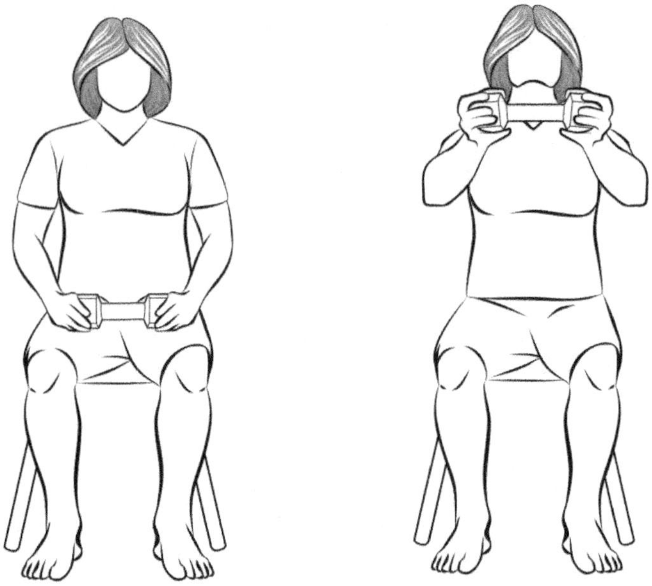

1. **Sit tall** in your chair with your seat toward the back of the chair. **Engage your core** throughout this exercise. Place your feet flat on the floor and your shoulders straight.
2. Hold the ends of one weight with both hands and place the weight on your lap. Breathe in.
3. Breathe out and slowly raise the weight, using both hands, to eye level.
4. Breathe in, and slowly lower your hands to the starting position. Feel your core muscles engage as you focus on sitting tall.

5. Start with 10 repetitions. Gradually build up to 3 sets or 30 repetitions.

Slowly ramp up:

Once you have the correct technique and you feel confident, try increasing the weight. So, if you started with a 2-lb weight, do the exercises with a 3-lb weight, and so on.

Caution:

Stop immediately if this exercise causes you pain. Lift your arms as high as you can without causing pain. You should be able to slowly increase the degree of the lift as you get stronger. You can also try using a lower pound weight or doing the exercise without weights; use your clenched fists instead. If you still feel pain, skip this exercise and come back to it when you have more strength and flexibility.

Bicep Curl

Position: Seated

Equipment Needed: Weights

Primary Area(s) Worked: Biceps

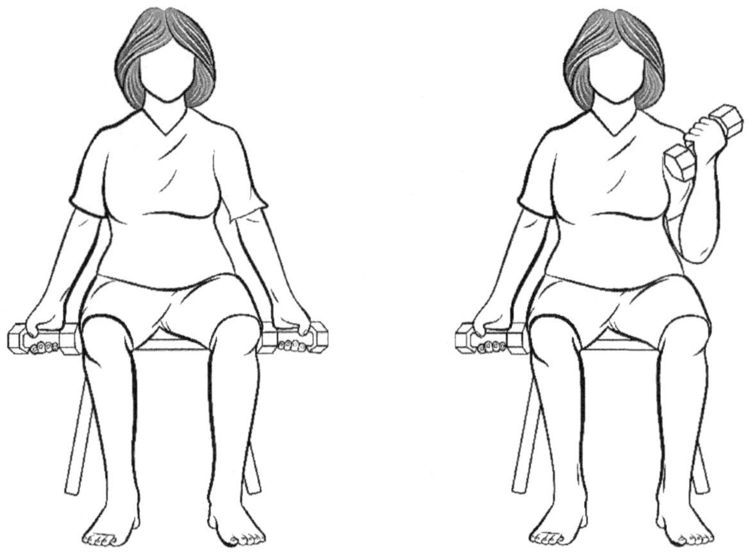

1. **Sit tall** with your seat toward the back of the chair. Your feet should be flat on the floor. **Engage your core** throughout the exercise.
2. Hold a weight in each hand, with your palms facing up. Drop your arms to your side.
3. Keep your elbows close to your side. If you are in a chair with arms, rest your hands in your lap as your starting position. Breathe in.
4. Breathe out and slowly bring your right arm up to your chest. Feel the muscle in your bicep tighten.

5. Breathe in and slowly bring your arm back to your starting position.
6. Breathe out and slowly bring your left arm up to your chest. Feel the muscle in your bicep tighten.
7. Breathe in and slowly bring your arm back to your starting position.
8. Keep your core engaged and your shoulders relaxed as you perform these exercises.
9. Start with 10 repetitions on both arms. Gradually build up to 3 sets or 30 repetitions.

Slowly ramp up:

Once you have the correct technique and you feel confident, try increasing the weight. So, if you started with a 2-lb weight, do the exercises with a 3-lb weight, and so on.

Caution:

Stop immediately if this exercise causes you pain. Lift your arms as high as you can without causing pain. You should be able to slowly increase the degree of the lift as you get stronger. You can also try using a lower pound weight or doing the exercise without weights; use your clenched fists instead. If you still feel pain, skip this exercise and come back to it when you have more strength and flexibility.

Bicep Strengthening

Position: Standing

Equipment Needed: Chair

Primary Area(s) Worked: Biceps

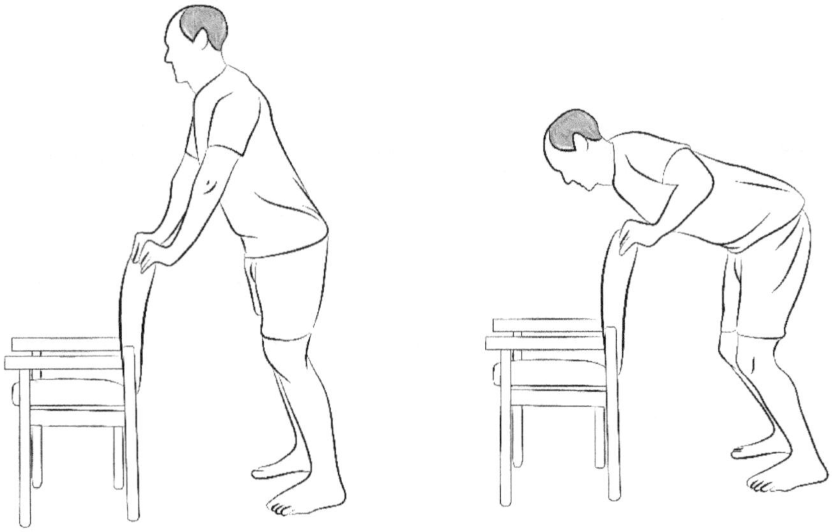

1. Stand behind a sturdy chair that will not slide or stand next to a counter.
2. Place both hands on the back of the chair or counter. Slightly bend your knees. Breathe in.
3. **Engage your core.** Keeping your back straight, use your biceps muscles to slowly lower your chest and upper torso down over the chair or counter. Breathe out as you lower your body.
4. Breathe in and use your biceps to slowly raise your body back to the starting position. Your back and upper torso should remain straight.

5. Start with 10 repetitions. Gradually build up to 3 sets or 30 repetitions.

Slowly ramp up:

Once you have the correct technique and feel confident, increase the repetitions.

Caution:

If doing this exercise causes you pain, stop. Lower your torso as far as you can without causing pain. You should be able to slowly increase the degree of the lift as you get stronger. If you still feel pain, skip this exercise for now and come back to it when you have more strength and flexibility.

Triceps Curl 

Position: Seated

Equipment Needed: Weights

Primary Area(s) Worked: Triceps

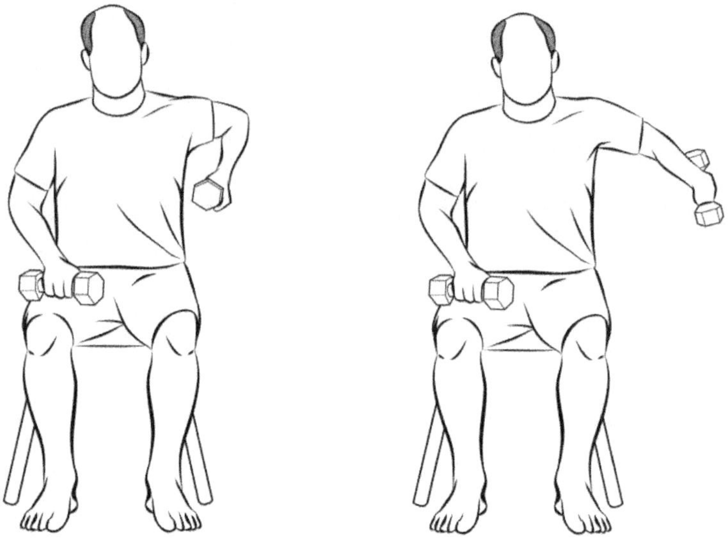

1. **Sit tall**, leaning slightly forward in the chair. **Engage your core** throughout the exercise. Your feet should be flat on the floor. Your shoulders should be positioned up and slightly back. Retain this shoulder position throughout the exercise.
2. Hold a weight in each hand, with your palms facing down. Drop your arms to your side or on your thighs. Bend the elbow slightly. Breathe in.
3. Breathe out and using your shoulder muscle, slowly raise your right arm out and angled back to shoulder height.

4. Breathe in and using your shoulder muscle, gently release your arm back to the starting position. Continue to keep your shoulders up and slightly back.
5. Repeat this exercise using your left arm.
6. Start with 10 repetitions on both arms. Gradually build up to 3 sets or 30 repetitions.

Slowly ramp up:

Once you have the correct technique and you feel confident, try increasing the weight. So, if you started with a 2-lb weight, do the exercises with a 3-lb weight, and so on.

Caution:

Stop immediately if this exercise causes you pain. Bring your arms as far back as you can without causing pain. You should be able to slowly increase the degree of the lift as you get stronger. You can also try using a lower pound weight or doing the exercise without weights; use your clenched fists instead. If you still feel pain, skip this exercise and come back to it when you have more strength and flexibility.

Triceps Push

Position: Seated

Equipment Needed: None

Primary Area(s) Worked: Triceps

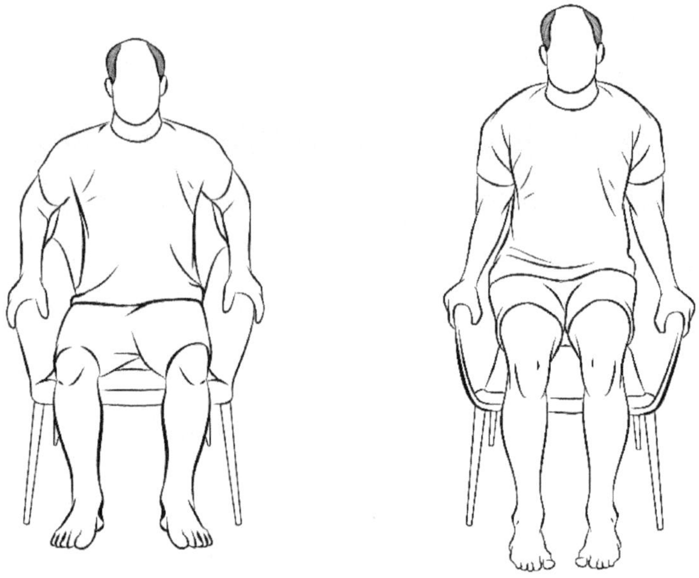

1. **Sit tall** in your chair with your chest out. **Engage your core** throughout the exercise.
2. Place your hands on the arms of the chair. Breathe in.
3. Breathe out, and, using only your arms, push up in the chair.
4. Breathe in, and, using only your arms, lower your body back to the starting position.
5. Start with 10 repetitions on both arms. Gradually build up to 3 sets or 30 repetitions.

Slowly ramp up:

Once you have the correct technique and you feel confident, increase the number of repetitions, and pause for 3–5 seconds while you are in the up position.

Caution:

If doing this exercise causes you pain, stop. Try using your arms to raise your upper body as far as you can without causing pain. You should be able to slowly increase the amount you can raise your body as your upper body gets stronger. If you still feel pain, skip this exercise for now and come back to it when you have more strength and flexibility.

Elbow Extensions

Position: Seated or Standing

Equipment Needed: Optional Weights

Primary Area(s) Worked: Elbow, Forearm, Wrist

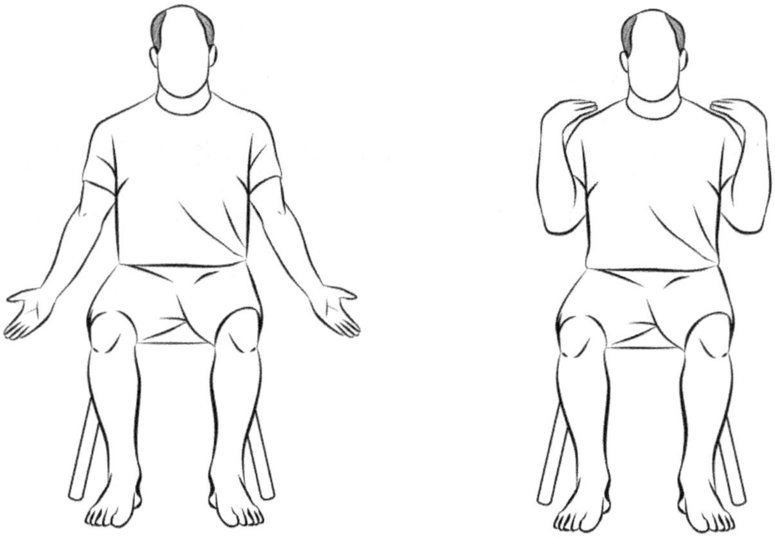

1. **Sit tall** in a chair with your shoulders back and your chest out. **Engage your core** throughout the exercise.
2. Extend your arms straight down and slightly forward. Breathe in.
3. Breathe out and slowly bring your arms up, keeping your arms as straight as you can, and touch your shoulders.
4. Breathe in and return your arms to the starting position. Keep your arms as straight as you can.
5. Start with 10 repetitions on both arms. Gradually build up to 3 sets or 30 repetitions.

Slowly ramp up:

Once you have the correct technique and you feel confident, hold a light weight in both hands, palms up and perform the exercise using the weights. Increase the weight as you progress. So, if you started with a 2 lb. weight, do the exercises with a 3 lb. weight, and so on.

Caution:

If doing this exercise causes you pain, stop. If your arm gets tired, rest a while and start again. If you still feel pain, skip this exercise and return to it when you have more strength and flexibility.

Strength Training – Core

Diaphragmatic Breathing

Position: Seated or Lying Down

Equipment Needed: None

Primary Area(s) Worked: Diaphragm

Lying Down Position

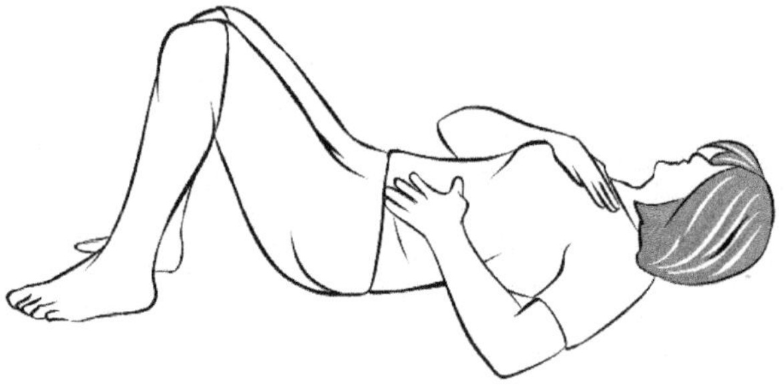

It is typically easier to start with this exercise lying down.

Lie on your back on a flat surface or in bed. Bend your knees and keep your feet flat on the surface. Support your head if it is more comfortable. Allow your body to relax.

Seated Position

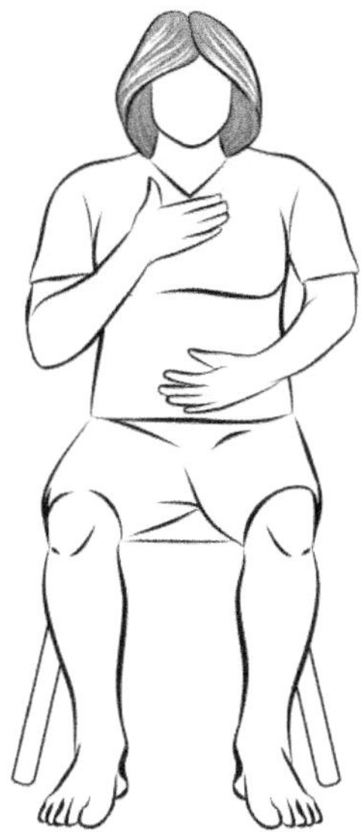

This position is more difficult as you are working against gravity.

Sit comfortably with your knees bent and your shoulders, head, and neck relaxed. Your feet should be firmly planted on the floor. Allow your body to relax.

Perform the Diaphragmatic Exercise

1. Place one hand on your upper chest and the other just below your rib cage. This will allow you to feel your diaphragm move as you breathe.
2. Breathe slowly through your nose so your stomach moves out, causing your hand to rise. The hand on your chest should remain as still as possible. If you feel the hand on your chest, or both the hand on your chest and your stomach moving, you are using muscles other than just the diaphragm for breathing.

3. Breathe out. Tighten your stomach muscles so that your stomach moves in, causing your hand to lower as you breathe out through pursed lips. **Engage Your Core.** The hand on your upper chest should remain as still as possible.
4. Start slowly doing this breathing exercise for 5–6 minutes. Repeat 3 or 4 times throughout the day.
5. Initially, you may get tired while doing this exercise. But keep at it. With continued practice, diaphragmatic breathing will become automatic.

Slowly ramp up:

Once you are comfortable with the exercise, gradually increase the time you spend doing it. You can also place a book on your abdomen while doing the exercise.

Caution:

If you have COPD, please discuss these exercises with your doctor before doing them. If you experience dizziness or excessive yawning, or your breathing feels mechanical, you may be over breathing or trying to force the breathing. If this happens, allow your body to relax and start over.

Pelvic Floor Kegels

Position: Seated or Lying Down

Equipment Needed: Optional Small Ball, Towels

Primary Area(s) Worked: Pelvic Floor

In 1950, Arnold Kegel, a gynecologist from the University of Southern California, discovered a simple exercise to build muscles along the pelvic floor. He found that squeezing and holding the pelvic muscles for several seconds, then releasing them, could strengthen these muscles and help control incontinence. This exercise sequence, which is for both men and women, is now known as Kegels. They can be done while lying down or sitting at a desk, driving your car, or even while you are watching TV.

Kegels for Women

Seated Position

1. Sit toward the front of the chair and lean forward slightly with your hands on your knees. Lift your chest up and your head up. Do not slump your body.
2. It may be helpful to sit on a towel that has been rolled up to about the width of your hand or a soft exercise ball, as these may help you feel the muscles in this area.
3. Lift your chest, keep the curve in your lower back and breathe normally.
4. Perform the Kegel exercise for women.

Lying Down Position

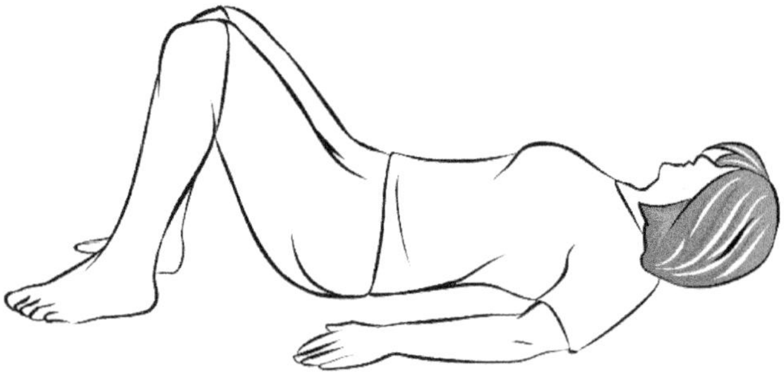

1. Lie down on the floor or on a firm bed, with your knees bent and about hip distance apart.
2. Be sure you have a curve in your back. Your back should not be flat on the floor.
3. Breathe normally.
4. Perform the Kegel exercise for women.

The Kegel Exercise for Women

1. Tighten your anus as if trying to stop gas from passing. Visualize lifting a marble in your anus. Your anus should tighten, but your buttocks should stay relaxed. If you feel yourself rising upward, you are using your buttocks. Keeping your anus closed, lift your anus up and inward as if you are pulling it up toward your navel. You should feel a squeezing feeling around your anus.
2. Squeeze the entrance to your vagina as if you are squeezing it shut. Visualize lifting a blueberry in your vagina. Keeping the vagina closed, draw it up and inward toward your navel.
3. Squeeze the area around the urinary opening as if stopping the urine flow. Visualize lifting a raisin in your urinary opening. Keeping the vagina closed, draw it up and inward toward your navel. Breathe in.
4. Breathe out and squeeze and lift the anus, vagina, and urethra simultaneously. Hold for 2–3 seconds. Breathe in as you slowly lower your body to the starting position. This process is one Kegel.
5. Rest for 5–10 seconds while breathing normally. Then do your next Kegel.
6. Start with 2–3 Kegels, with a 2–3 second hold. Do these three times per day. When you start, focus on feeling the muscles contract and release and doing the exercises correctly. Then ramp up.

Kegels for Men

Seated Position

Sit tall toward the front part of a chair. Lift your chest and your head up. Do not slump your body. This is a good position for beginners. Perform the Kegel exercise for men.

All Fours Position

Kneel on all fours with your knees bent and your forearms on the floor. Perform the Kegel exercise for men.

The Kegel Exercise for Men

1. Shorten or withdraw your penis inward toward your abdomen. Your scrotum moves slightly upward toward your body. This is a subtle movement, but if you hold your fingers around the base of your penis, you may feel the muscle that wraps around it move as you move your penis inward and toward your body.
2. Imagine that you are trying to stop or slow the flow of urine while contracting around the base of your penis.
3. Tighten your anus as if trying to stop gas from passing. Your anus should tighten, but your buttocks should stay relaxed. If you feel yourself rising upward, you are using your buttocks, not your pelvic floor muscles.
4. As you breathe out, shorten, and tighten the penis, squeeze to stop the urine flow, and tighten your anus simultaneously. You should feel your scrotum and abdomen rise slightly toward your body.
5. Hold for 2–3 second. As you breathe in, let these muscles relax and return to your resting position. This is one Kegel. Rest for 5–10 seconds and breathe normally before doing your next Kegel.
6. Start with 2–3 Kegels, with a 2–3 second hold. Do these three times per day. When you begin, focus on feeling the muscles contract and release and doing the exercises correctly before you ramp up.

Slowly ramp up:

Once you have the correct technique and are confident that you know how to do these exercises, increase the strength of the squeeze and the duration of the hold to 10 seconds. Increase the number of Kegels to 8–12, three times a day.

Caution:

The following guidelines that can help you avoid common mistakes:

- Do not do a Kegel while urinating.
- Do not go directly to the ramp-up number of Kegels each day. Start small.
- Do not do the lifting when you are running, walking, or doing other exercises. You will not be able to rest and relax in between, which is essential.
- When starting, do not contract too strongly. It is important to first master the technique and feel the muscles contract.
- Do not hold your breath. It is important to breathe as described during your exercise.
- Do not tense your abdominal muscles. They should be relaxed when doing the Kegel exercises.

Dolphin Kick

Position: Lying Down

Equipment Needed: None

Primary Area(s) Worked: Abdomen

1. Start this exercise by lying on your back on the floor or on a firm bed.
2. Bring your knees up, pointed toward the ceiling. Keep your arms out beside you.
3. Breathe in and bring your knees in toward your chest.

4. **Engage your core** and straighten both legs up toward the ceiling.
5. Breathe out as you bring both legs down until midway from the ceiling to the ground.
6. Hold for 2–3 seconds. Your navel should be in toward your spine.
7. Bring both legs back into the chest.
8. Start with 10 repetitions. Gradually build up to 3 sets or 30 repetitions.

Slowly ramp up:

Once you have the correct technique and feel confident, slow the time you lower your legs to the midway position and hold the position for 5–6 seconds. Then slow the time that you bring your knees to your chest.

Caution:

If doing this exercise causes you pain, stop. If you have a high level of bone loss, or your back, hips, or legs are sensitive, try bringing one leg partially down, with a slight knee bend, then bring the other leg down to match the first leg. Then draw your knees back into your chest area. If you still feel pain, skip this exercise and return to it when you have more strength and flexibility.

Leg Extension 

Position: Lying Down

Equipment Needed: Optional Small Ball

Primary Area(s) Worked: Abdomen

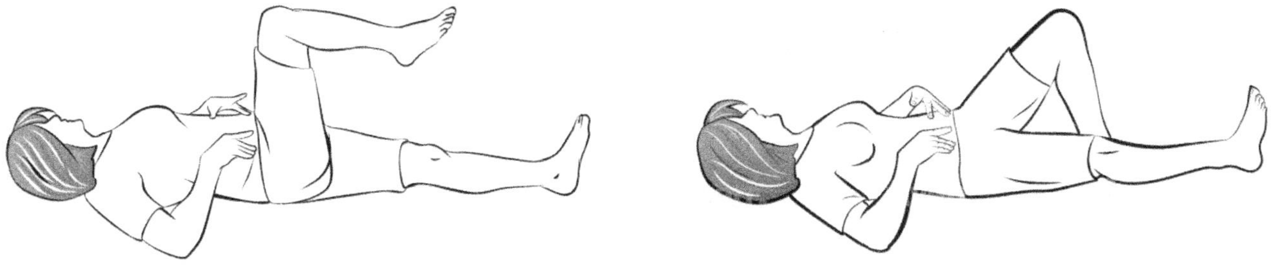

1. Start this exercise by lying on your back on the floor or on a firm bed. Be sure you have a little space between your lower back and the flat surface.
2. **Engage your core**. Breathe in.
3. Keeping your hips stable, breathe out and bring your right knee pointed toward the ceiling, and then slowly extend your right leg out a few inches off the floor. Bring your rib cage down to the floor. Ensure your hips remain firmly on the floor and your entire abdomen contracted.
4. Breathe in as you slowly bring your right leg back in.
5. Repeat with your left leg, paying close attention to your breathing and keeping your core engaged.

6. Start with 10 repetitions on each leg. Gradually build up to 3 sets or 30 repetitions.

Slowly ramp up:

Once you have the correct technique and feel confident, put a child's ball between your knees and squeeze your knees into the ball. Contract your abdominal muscle to keep your core engaged. Continue to squeeze the ball between your knees, breathing out as you bring both knees up toward the ceiling. Keep the core engaged and breathe in as you lower your knees to the floor. Repeat.

Caution:

Stop doing this exercise immediately if you feel pain. If this is too difficult, or if you feel any discomfort in your lower back, try raising your legs as far as you can without causing pain. You should be able to slowly raise them higher as you get stronger. If this is too difficult or you feel any discomfort in your lower back, only do the breathing and abdominal muscle contractions. If you still feel pain, skip this exercise and return to it when you have more strength and flexibility.

Dead Bug

Position: Lying Down

Equipment Needed: Weights

Primary Area(s) Worked: Abdomen

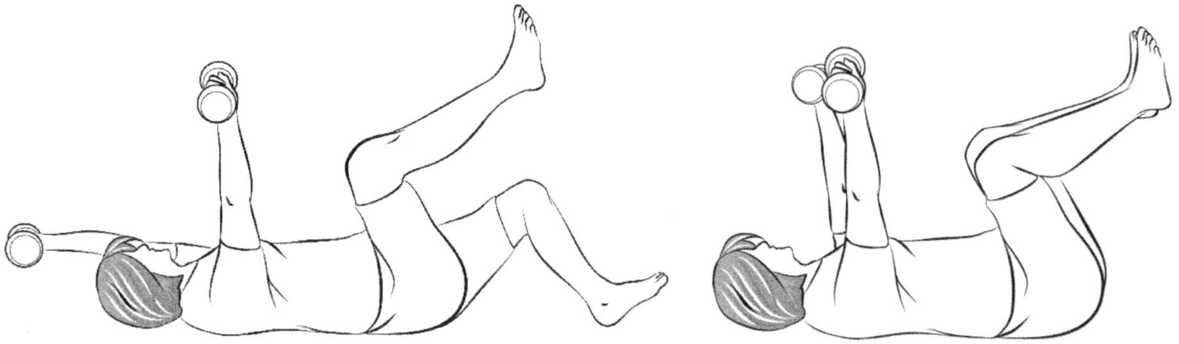

1. Start this exercise by lying on your back on the floor or on a firm bed. Hold a small weight in each hand.
2. Breathe in and bring both arms and legs toward the ceiling.
3. Breathe out, **engage your core,** and bring your right arm and left leg down to the floor.
4. Breathe in as you bring the right arm and leg back up.
5. Breathe out while engaging your core and bring your left arm and right leg down to the floor. Breathe in and bring the same limbs back up.
6. Start with 10 repetitions on each leg. Gradually build up to 3 sets or 30 repetitions.

Slowly ramp up:

Once you have the correct technique and you feel confident, try increasing the weight. So, if you started with a 2-lb weight, do the exercises with a 3-lb weight, and so on.

Caution:

If doing this exercise causes you pain, stop. If this is too difficult, or if you feel any discomfort in your lower back, try raising your legs only as far as is comfortable, and lowering your arms to the comfortable point. You can also try using a lower pound weight or doing the exercise without weights; use your clenched fists instead. If you still feel pain, skip this exercise and come back to it when you have more strength and flexibility.

Reverse Crunch

Position: Lying Down

Equipment Needed: Optional Weights

Primary Area(s) Worked: Abdomen

1. Start this exercise by lying on your back on the floor or on a firm bed.
2. Place your hands behind your head and cradle your head in your hands. Your head should be off the floor about an inch.
3. **Engage your core.** Breathe in.
4. Breathe out as you bring your right leg toward your chest and extend your left leg out. At the same time, bring your left elbow slightly toward your right knee. Make a slight rotation but be careful not to twist your spine.
5. Breathe in as you return to the center and reverse your position.
6. Breathe out as you bring your left leg toward your chest and extend your right leg out. At the same time, bring your right elbow slightly toward your left knee. Make a slight rotation when bringing the elbows to the knees but be careful not to twist your spine.

7. Start with 10 repetitions, where one repetition extends and brings each leg back to the center. Gradually build up to 3 sets or 30 repetitions.

Slowly ramp up:

Once you have the correct technique and feel confident, hold a small weight in each hand and place your hands on the side of your head. Instead of bringing your elbow to your knee, try to touch the weight to your knee.

Caution:

If doing this exercise causes you pain, stop. If this is too difficult, or if you have significant bone loss in your back, raise your legs higher toward the ceiling, and be very careful not to twist your back. If you still feel pain, skip this exercise and return to it when you have more strength and flexibility.

Plank

Position: Lying Down

Equipment Needed: None

Primary Area(s) Worked: Abdomen

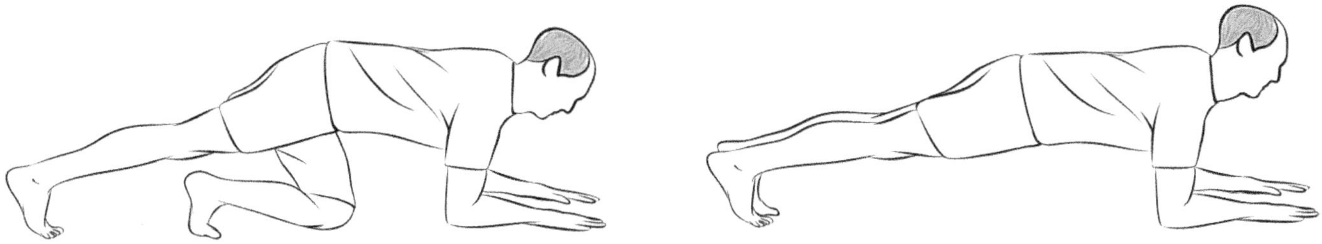

1. Start this exercise by lying on your stomach on the floor or on a firm bed.
2. Raise your chest up onto your elbows. Your elbows should be directly under your shoulders.
3. **Engage your core.**
4. Raise up on one knee, then extend both legs behind you. Your legs should be resting on your toes.
5. It should feel as if your abdominal muscles are pressing up toward the ceiling. Press your navel toward your spine. Your neck, back, and hips should be in a straight line. Do not let your hips sag downward to extend upward. Face straight ahead. Do not let your neck and head droop downward.
6. Breathe in.

7. Slowly breathe out as you hold this position for 10 seconds. Breathe in and slowly lower your legs to where they are resting on your knees.
8. Start with 10 repetitions. Gradually build up to 3 sets or 30 repetitions.

Slowly ramp up:

Once you have the correct technique and feel confident, try increasing the hold time. You can also increase the repetitions.

Caution:

If doing this exercise causes you pain, stop. If this is too difficult, try doing a modified plank. Lift your torso onto your elbows. Keep your knees on the ground and gently raise up on your arms. Keep your head and back in alignment. Breathe out, press your navel to your spine, and hold for 10 seconds. Lower your upper body and repeat. If you still feel pain, skip this exercise and return to it when you have more strength and flexibility.

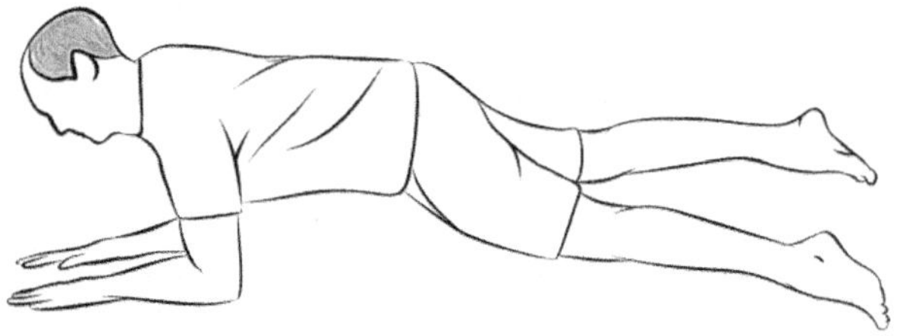

Bridge

Position: Lying Down

Equipment Needed: Optional Weights

Primary Area(s) Worked: Lower Back, Glutes, Hips

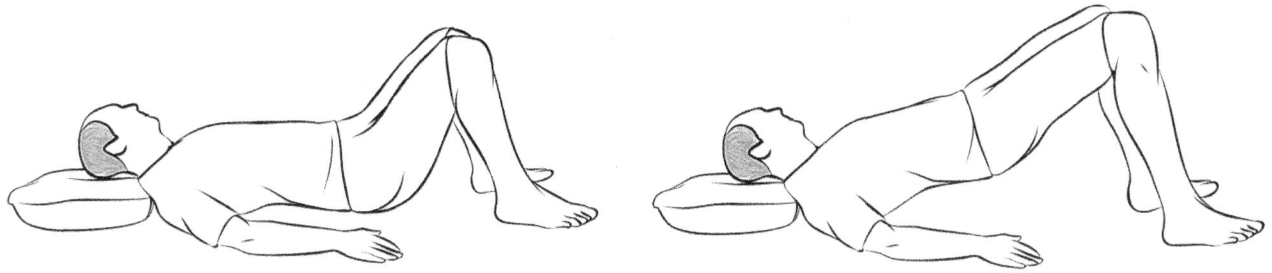

1. Start this exercise by lying on your back on the floor or on a firm bed. Use a pillow or folded towels to support your head and upper back if needed.
2. Place your hands by your side and raise your knees. Keep your knees close to your body.
3. Visualize squeezing your buttock muscles together as if squeezing a dollar bill between your buttocks. Breathe in.
4. Breathe out, press down with your hands, and lift your buttocks toward the ceiling. Your buttock muscles should be contracting. Push your toes out. Lift your buttocks as high as you comfortably can without pain. The objective is to form a straight line between your shoulders and the tops of your knees.
5. Hold for 2–3 seconds, squeezing your buttocks.

6. Breathe in as you slowly lower your buttocks back down.
7. Start with 10 repetitions. Gradually build up to 3 sets or 30 repetitions.

Slowly ramp up:

Once you have the correct technique and feel confident, you can add some weights. Start by putting a 1- to 2-lb weight on your pelvis area. Then slowly lift and lower your buttocks as before. Gradually increase the weight until it is no longer comfortable for you to complete the exercise.

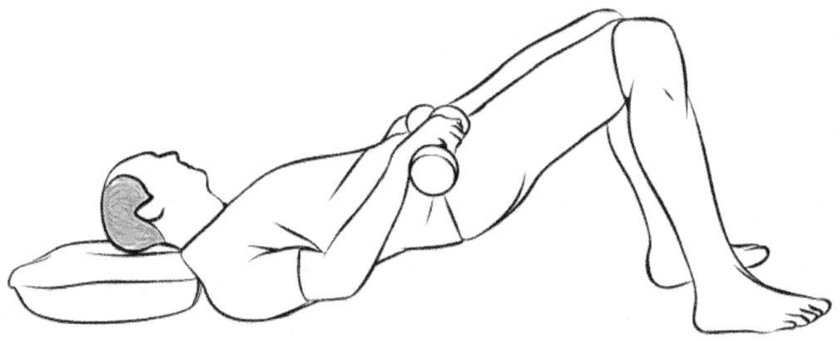

Caution:

If doing this exercise causes you pain, stop. Try lowering the amount that you lift your buttocks. It is OK to start with shallow buttock raises and work up. If you still feel pain, skip this exercise and return to it when you have more strength and flexibility.

Extended Bridge

Position: Lying Down

Equipment Needed: None

Primary Area(s) Worked: Lower Back, Glutes, Hips

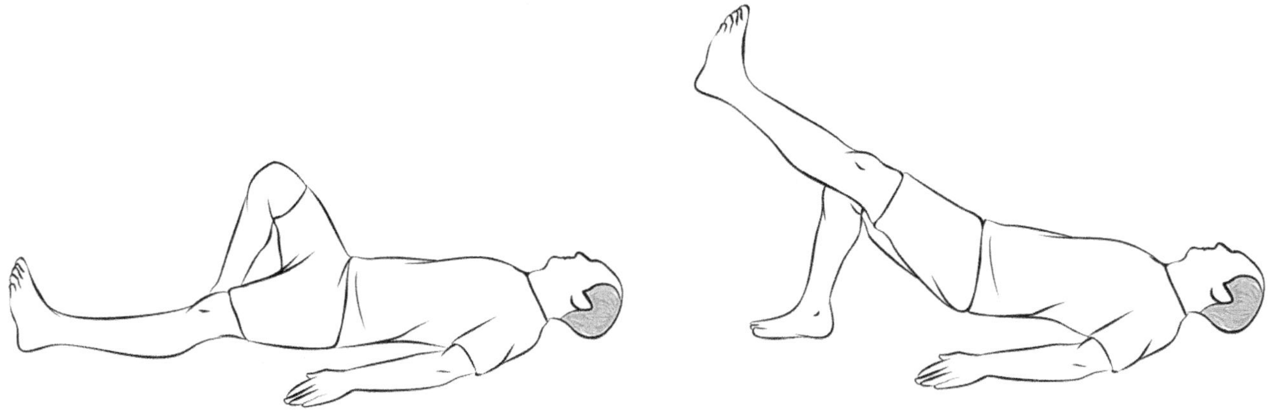

1. Start this exercise by lying on your back on the floor or on a firm bed. Use a pillow or folded towels to support your head and upper back if needed.
2. Place your hands by your side and bend your left knee.
3. Visualize squeezing your buttock muscles together as if squeezing a dollar bill between your buttocks. Breathe in.
4. Press down with your hands, and as you breathe out, slowly lift your right leg toward the ceiling as far as comfortable. Hold for 2–3 seconds.
5. Breathe in and lower your right leg to the starting position. Repeat the sequence 10 times.

6. Do the same sequence with the other leg. Bend your right knee and extend your left leg. Repeat 10 times.
7. Start with 10 repetitions for each leg. Gradually build up to 3 sets or 30 repetitions.

Slowly ramp up:

Gradually increase the number of repetitions.

Caution:

If doing this exercise causes you pain, stop. Try lowering the amount that you lift your leg. It is OK to start with a lower leg lift and work up. If you need more support, you can put your extended leg on a chair for 2–3 seconds before lowering it down to the starting position. If you still feel pain, skip this exercise and return to it when you have more strength and flexibility.

Clam

Position: Lying Down

Equipment needed: Optional Weights

Primary Area(s) Worked: Hips

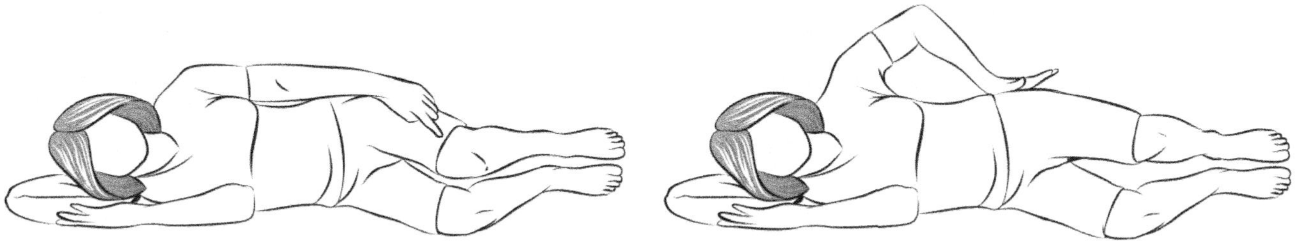

1. Start this exercise by lying on your right side on the floor or on a firm bed. Use a pillow or folded towels to support your head and upper back if needed.
2. Bend your knees forward slightly, feet together. Make sure your knees are in alignment when you look down.
3. Breathe in and slowly lift your top knee away from the lower knee. Keep your feet together.
4. Lift to a count of two, then breathe out as you slowly lower the knee to a count of four.
5. Keep your spine straight when lifting your knee. Rest your outer hand on your hip area to feel the muscle contract. Be sure you are not rotating your spine.
6. Start with 10 repetitions and gradually build up to 3 sets or 30 repetitions.

7. Turn around so you are lying on your left side and repeat the sequence working your left hip.
8. Start with 10 repetitions and gradually build up to 3 sets or 30 repetitions.

Slowly ramp up:

Once you have the correct technique and feel confident, you can add some weights. Start by putting a 1- to 2-lb weight on your leg just above the knee and executing the lift sequence. Gradually increase the weight until it is no longer comfortable for you to complete the exercise.

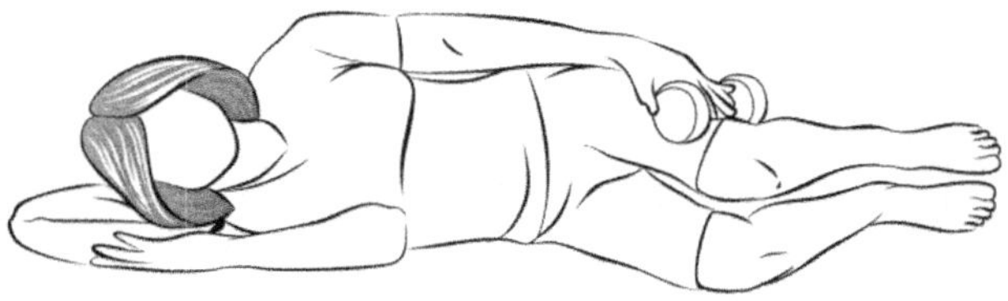

Caution:

If doing this exercise causes you pain, stop. Try reducing the amount that you raise your knee. Also, check your alignment. You should be able to look down and see the top of your knees. Your lift movement must be straight up without rotating the spine. If you still feel pain, skip this exercise and return to it when you have more strength and flexibility.

Side Leg Lift

Position: Lying Down

Equipment Needed: Optional Weights

Primary Area(s) Worked: Hips

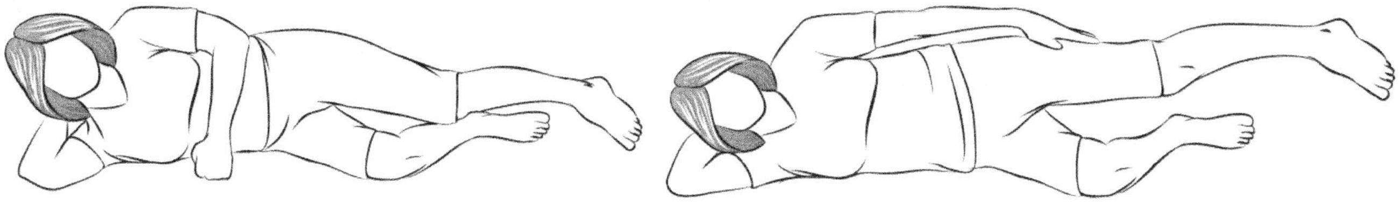

1. Start this exercise by lying on your right side on the floor or on a firm bed. Use a pillow or folded towels to support your head and upper back if needed.
2. Bend your knees forward slightly, feet together. Move your lower leg back, still slightly bent.
3. Breathe in and extend your top leg and point your toe downward.
4. Breathe out and slowly lift your top leg until it is about parallel with the rest of your body.
5. Lift to a count of two. Hold for 2–3 seconds, then breathe in and slowly lower it to the ground to a count of four.
6. Start with 10 repetitions and gradually build up to 3 sets or 30 repetitions.

7. Turn around so you are lying on your left side and repeat the sequence.
8. Start with 10 repetitions and gradually build up to 3 sets or 30 repetitions.

Slowly ramp up:

Once you have the correct technique and feel confident, you can add some weights. Start by putting a 1- to 2-lb weight on your leg just above the knee and executing the lift sequence. Gradually increase the weight until it is no longer comfortable for you to complete the exercise.

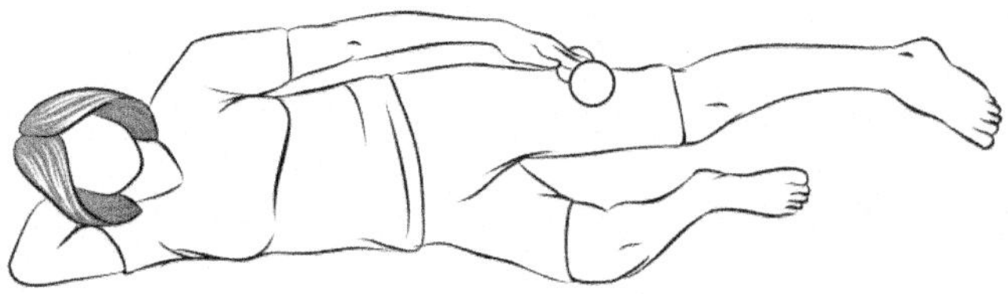

Caution:

If doing this exercise causes you pain, stop. Try reducing the amount that you raise your leg. Also, check your alignment. If you still feel pain, skip this exercise and return to it when you have more strength and flexibility.

Flutter Kick

Position: Lying Down

Equipment Needed: None

Primary Area(s) Worked: Lower Back, Glutes, Hips

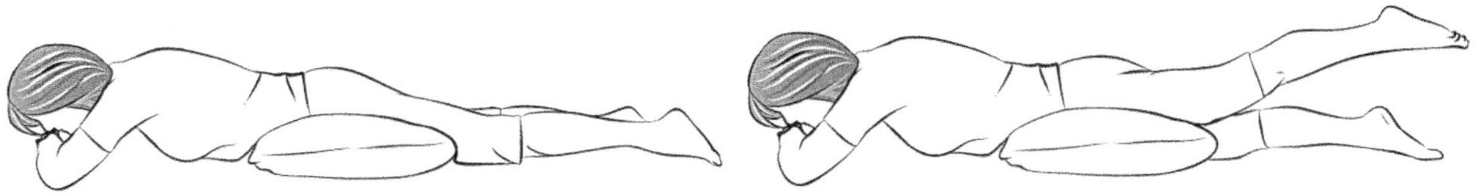

1. Start this exercise by lying on your stomach on the floor or on a firm bed. Use a pillow or folded towels to support your head and upper back if needed.
2. Place a pillow or folded towels under your hips to support your back and pelvis. You can use two pillows if it is more comfortable for you.
3. Fold your hands in front of your forehead and place your forehead on your hands. If this is uncomfortable for you, you can also place your arms beside you.
4. Breathe in.
5. Squeeze your buttocks, pull your shoulders toward your ears, breathe out, and slowly raise your right leg a few inches off the ground. Raise to a count of two. Hold for 2–3 seconds, then breathe in and slowly lower it to the ground to a count of four.

6. Start with 10 repetitions and gradually build up to 3 sets or 30 repetitions.
7. Perform the routine on the left leg.
8. Repeat the repetitions as above.

Slowly ramp up:

Perform the exercise as described above, with the following exception. As you raise your right leg off the ground, slightly raise and extend your left arm, thumb up, out in front of you. Slowly bring your arm down as you slowly lower your right leg. Repeat with the other leg and arm.

Caution:

If doing this exercise causes you pain, stop. Try using another pillow or additional towels and/or lowering the amount you raise. If you still feel pain, skip this exercise and return to it when you have more strength and flexibility.

Strength Building – Lower Body

The following exercises are excellent for building strength in your lower body. You can also do the balance exercises in Chapter 12 to help build lower leg strength.

Modified Heel Drops

Position: Standing

Equipment Needed: None

Primary Area(s) Worked: Lower Back, Hips, Calves, Ankles

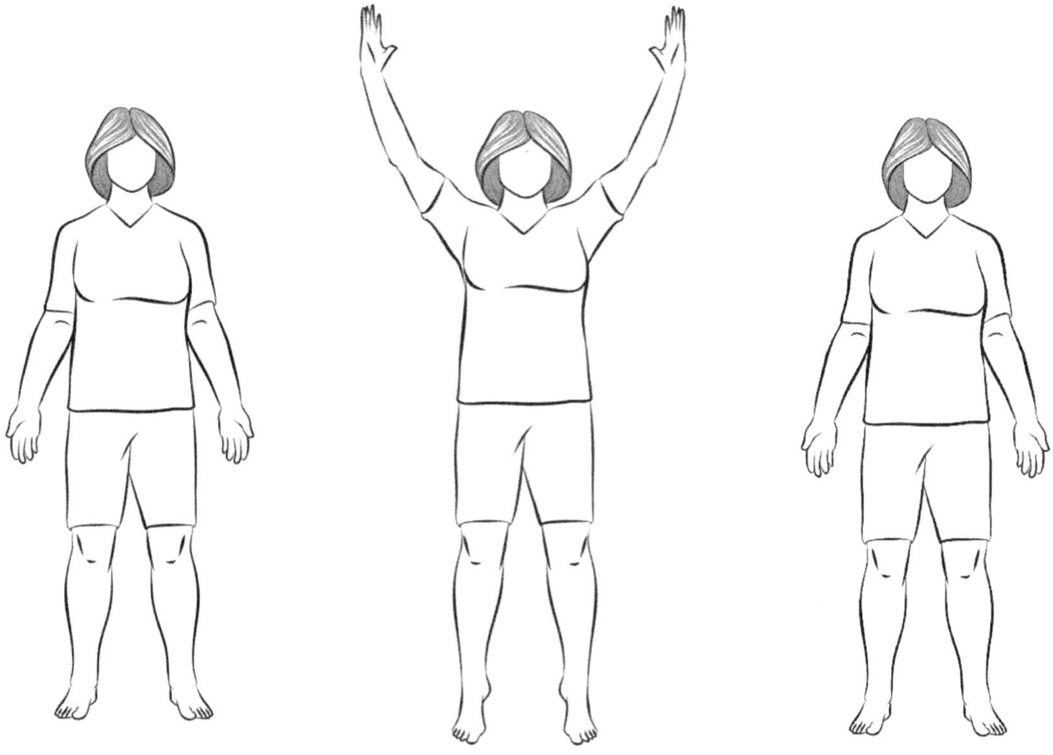

1. Use the back of a sturdy chair or countertop for support if needed.
2. Stand with your feet about hip-width apart and your knees slightly bent. Your hands should be loosely at your sides.
3. Lift your heels as high as possible so that your weight is on your toes. At the same time, raise both hands to the sky.
4. Hold for 3 seconds.
5. Then quickly lower your heels to the ground and drop your hands to your sides.
6. Start with 10 repetitions. Gradually build up to 3 sets or 30 repetitions.

Slowly ramp up:

Slowly increase the number of repetitions. As you lower your heels, bend your knees slightly so that you are lowering into a slight squat position.

Caution:

If doing this exercise causes you pain, stop. If you have balance issues, be sure you are using the chair, counter, or furniture for support. Try lowering the level that you lift your heels off the ground and try again. If you still feel pain, skip this exercise and return to it when you have more strength and flexibility.

Inner Thigh Lifts 

Position: Lying Down

Equipment Needed: Optional Ankle Weight

Primary Area(s) Worked: Thighs

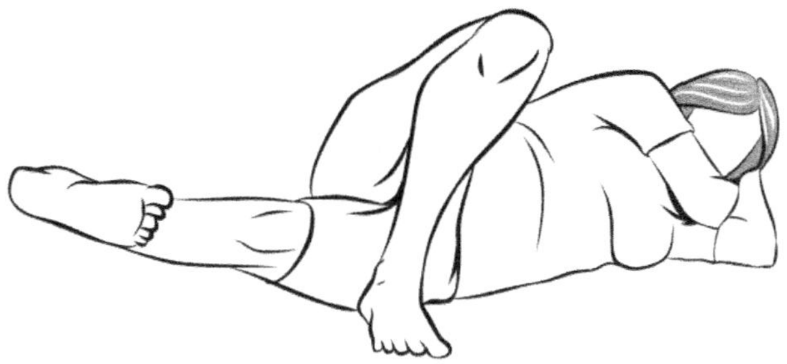

1. Start by lying on your right side on the floor or bed.
2. Your right leg should be straight on the floor, with your toes straight up. Bend your left knee and place it in front of the right leg. Breathe in.
3. Breathe out as you slowly lift your right leg 3–5 inches off the floor or bed. Hold for 3–5 seconds.
4. Breathe in as you slowly lower your leg.
5. Perform this exercise 10 times with your right leg.
6. Perform the same exercise with the right knee bent and the left leg extended.
7. Gradually build up to 3 sets or 30 repetitions.

Slowly ramp up:

Once you have the correct technique and feel confident, you can add an ankle weight. Start by putting a 1- to 2-lb ankle weight on the leg you are lifting. Place it just below the calf. Gradually increase the weight until it is no longer comfortable for you to complete the exercise.

Caution:

If doing this exercise causes you pain, stop. Try resting between each leg lift or reducing the number of lifts in a repletion. If you still feel pain, skip this exercise.

Outer Thigh Lifts

Position: Lying Down

Equipment Needed: Optional Ankle Weight

Primary Area(s) Worked: Thighs

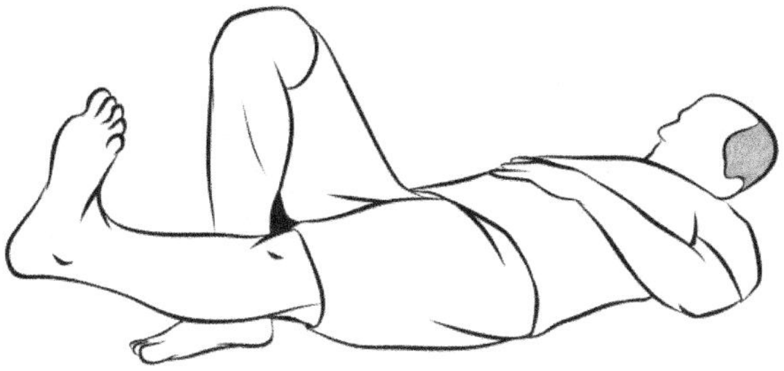

1. Start by lying on your back on the floor or on your bed.
2. Your right leg should be straight with your toes pointed upward. Your left knee is bent.
3. Tighten the muscle in your right thigh so that you can feel the muscle. Keep your right knee straight with your toes pointing upward. Breathe in.
4. Breathe out and slowly lift your right leg about 3–5 inches off the floor or bed. If you lift higher, the exercise will not target the correct muscles. Lift and hold for 3–4 seconds.
5. Breathe in and lower your leg back to the floor/bed.
6. Perform this exercise 10 times on your right leg.

7. Switch positions and extend your left leg out. Bend your right knee.
8. Perform this exercise 10 times on your left leg.
9. Gradually build up to 3 sets or 30 repetitions.

Slowly ramp up:

Once you have the correct technique and feel confident, you can add an ankle weight. Start by putting a 1- to 2-lb ankle weight on the leg you are lifting. Place it just below the calf. Gradually increase the weight until it is no longer comfortable for you to complete the exercise.

Caution:

If doing this exercise causes you pain, stop. Try resting between each leg lift, reducing the number of lifts in a repletion, or reducing the time you hold your leg up. If you still feel pain, skip this exercise and return to it when you have more strength and flexibility.

Seated March

Position: Seated

Equipment Needed: Optional Ankle Weights

Primary Area(s) Worked: Thighs and Lower Legs

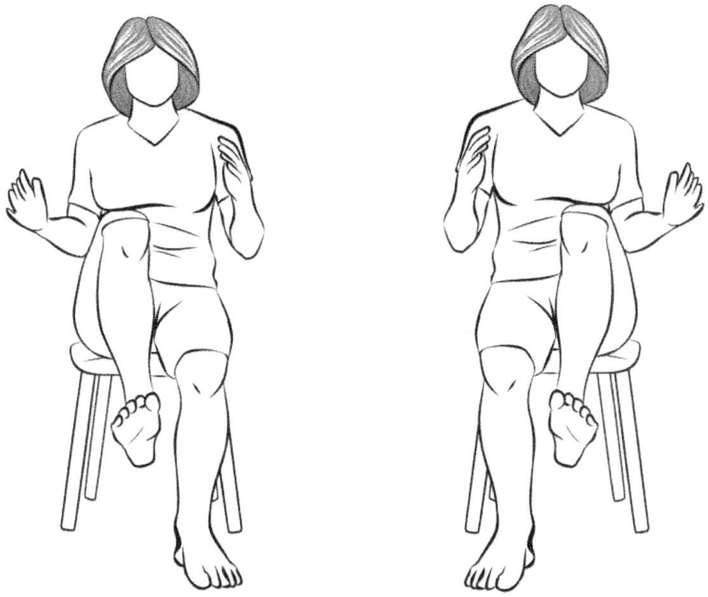

1. **Sit tall** in a chair with your feet on the floor. Maintain good alignment with your head, shoulders, and hips.
2. Bend your arms and bring your hands to chest height.
3. **Engage your core** and lift one knee toward your chest.
4. Lower your foot back down to the starting position and repeat the movement with the other leg. The movements should be at a comfortable pace.
5. Perform 10 repetitions on each leg.

6. Gradually build up to 3 sets or 30 repetitions.

Slowly ramp up:

Once you have the correct technique and feel confident, increase the number of repetitions and the speed of your movements. You can also add ankle weights. Start by putting a 1- to 2-lb ankle weight each leg. Place it just below the calf. Gradually increase the weight until it is no longer comfortable for you to complete the exercise.

Caution:

Stop immediately if this exercise causes you pain. Try reducing the height to which you raise your knee. Slower the pace and rest between sets. If you still feel pain, skip this exercise and return to it when you have more strength and flexibility.

Wall Squats

Position: Standing

Equipment Needed: Optional Small Ball

Primary Area(s) Worked: Thighs

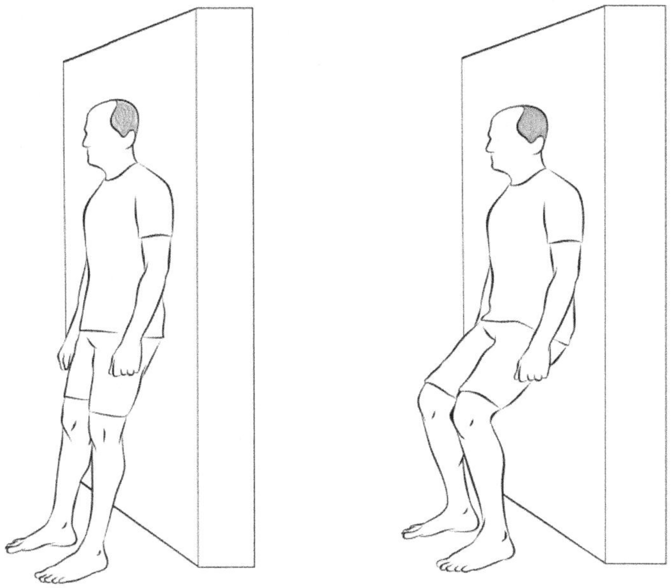

1. Stand against a wall, with your feet in front of you, about 2 feet away from the wall.
2. Keep your knees behind your toes. Breathe in.
3. Breathe out and slowly slide down the wall until you feel the muscles in your thighs tightening.
4. Hold for 5–10 seconds.
5. Breathe in and return to your starting position.
6. Start with 10 repetitions. Gradually build up to 3 sets or 30 repetitions.

Slowly ramp up:

Once you have the correct technique and feel confident, place a small exercise ball between your knees and gently squeeze the ball as you slide down the wall. Hold the squat for a longer time.

Caution:

If doing this exercise causes you pain, stop. Try readjusting your stance with your feet a little closer to the wall and/or not lowering as far down the wall. Be sure to check your knee position. If you still feel pain, skip this exercise and return to it when you have more strength and flexibility.

Seated Leg Lifts

Position: Seated

Equipment Needed: Optional Ankle Weight

Primary Area(s) Worked: Thighs

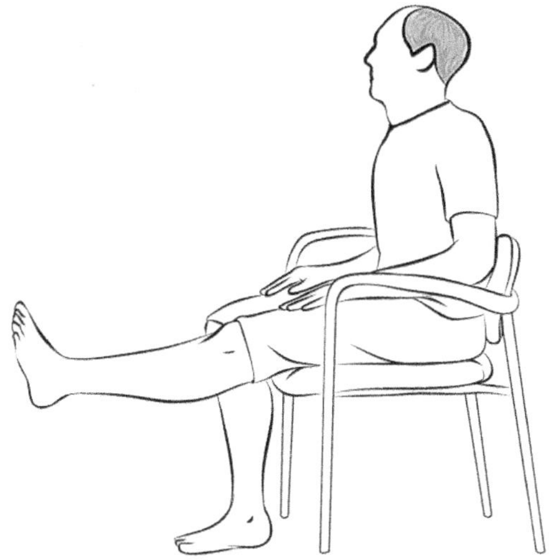

1. **Sit tall** with your seat toward the back of a chair. Breathe in.
2. With your thighs supported on the chair, breathe out and slowly lift your right leg to chair height.
3. Straighten your leg and hold for 3–5 seconds.
4. As you breathe in, slowly lower your leg.
5. Perform this exercise 10 times with your right leg.
6. Switch positions and extend your left leg out.
7. Perform this exercise 10 times with your left leg.
8. Gradually build up to 3 sets or 30 repetitions.

Slowly ramp up:

Once you have the correct technique and feel confident, you can add some weights. Start by putting a 1- to 2-lb ankle weight on the leg you are lifting. Place it just below the calf. Gradually increase the weight until it is no longer comfortable for you to complete the exercise.

Caution:

If doing this exercise causes you pain, stop. Try resting between each leg lift or reducing the number of lifts in a repletion. If you still feel pain, skip this exercise and return to it when you have more strength and flexibility.

Standing Heel Raises

Position: Standing

Equipment Needed: None

Primary Area(s) Worked: Thighs, Ankles, and Feet

1. **Stand tall** behind a chair, holding on to the back of the chair for support.
2. Bend your left knee at a 90-degree angle.
3. Slowly lift your right foot so that the weight is on the balls of your foot.
4. Hold for 3–5 seconds, then lower the foot.
5. Repeat 10 times.
6. Change legs and repeat lifting your left foot.
7. Repeat 10 times.
8. Gradually build up to 3 sets or 30 repetitions.

Slowly ramp up:

Once you have the correct technique and feel confident, increase the repetitions.

Caution:

If doing this exercise causes you pain, stop. Try reducing the amount that you bend your knee and/or lower the amount that you raise your foot. If you still feel pain, skip this exercise and return to it when you have more strength and flexibility.

Rolling Ball Massage

Position: Seated or Standing

Equipment needed: Tennis Ball

Primary Area(s) Worked: Feet, Heels, Arches

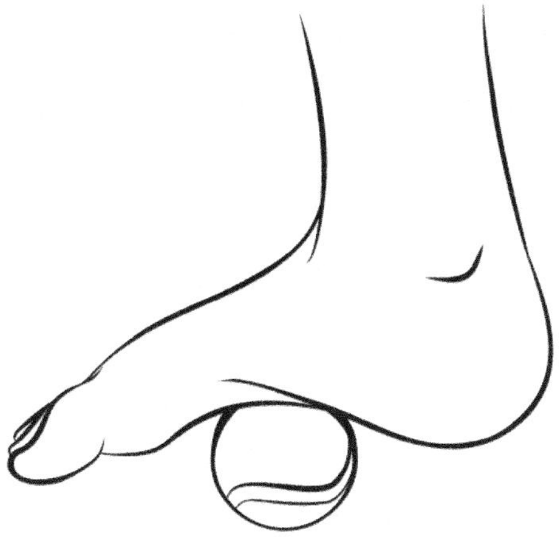

1. You can do this exercise standing or sitting. If you select the standing position, be sure to have a chair, counter, or piece of furniture for support should you need it.
2. Roll a tennis ball or similar size child's rubber ball slowly under your right foot. Roll the ball toward your toes and then back toward your heel. Use a pressure you are comfortable with.
3. Do this rolling motion 20 times. This is one rep.
4. Repeat this exercise on the left foot.
5. Do this exercise every day as often as you like.

Slowly ramp up:

If you want a deeper massage, try using a golf ball. You can also use a frozen water bottle wrapped in a towel.

Caution:

If doing this exercise causes you pain, stop. The bottoms of your feet may be sensitive at first. Reduce the pressure until the movement is comfortable, then gradually increase. If you still feel pain, skip this exercise and return to it when you have more strength and flexibility.

Tiptoe Walking

Position: Standing

Equipment Needed: None

Primary Area(s) Worked: Lower Legs (Calves and Shin), Ankles, Toes

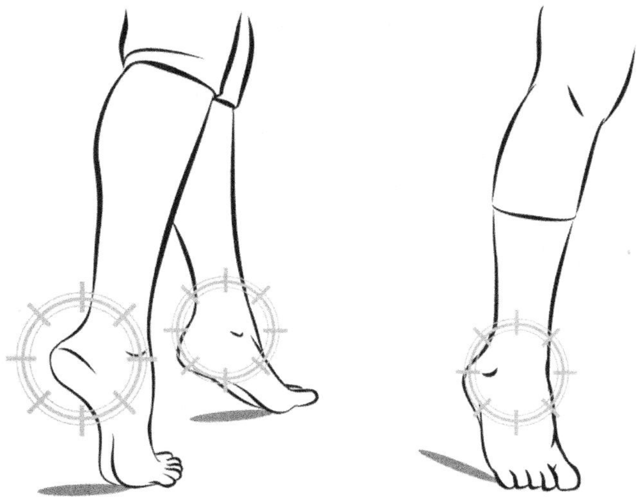

1. Tiptoe around your house. You can do this with shoes or with your bare feet.
2. Do this for 5–15 minutes, or until you get tired, and then rest.
3. Do this exercise 1–3 times a day.

Slowly ramp up:

Once you feel confident, increase the amount of time you do this exercise each day.

Caution:

If doing this exercise causes you pain, stop. Reduce the amount of time you do this exercise and gradually build up. If you have balance issues, be sure to do this exercise close to a counter, furniture, or other item providing support. If you still feel pain, skip this exercise and return to it when you have more strength and flexibility.

Ankle Flex

Position: Seated

Equipment Needed: None

Primary Area(s) Worked: Lower Legs and Ankles

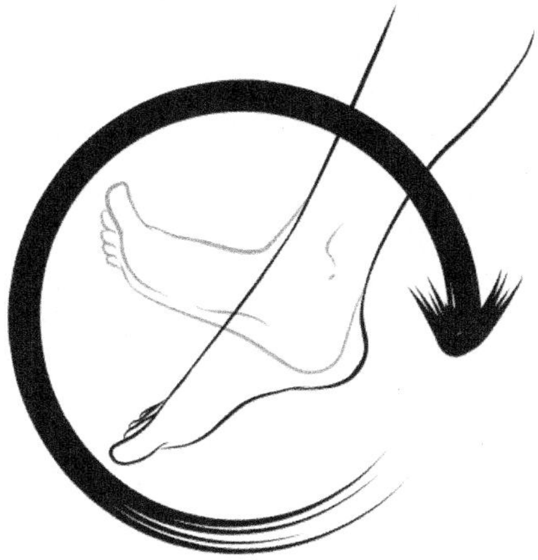

1. Start in a seated position.
2. Rotate your right foot in a circular motion.
3. Don't rush it. Do this exercise slowly.
4. Do 10 clockwise motions, then follow up with 10 counterclockwise movements. This is 1 rep.
5. Then do the same with your left foot.
6. Gradually build up to 3 sets, or 30 repetitions.

Slowly ramp up:

Once you have the correct technique and feel confident, increase the repetitions.

Caution:

If doing this exercise causes you pain, stop. Try reducing the number of repetitions and rest between them. If you still feel pain, skip this exercise and return to it when you have more strength and flexibility.

Toe Grabs

Position: Seated or Standing

Equipment Needed:

- A small hand towel
- A bowl
- A couple of small objects, such as a pencil or marble

Primary Area(s) Worked: Feet and Toes

1. You can do this exercise standing or sitting. If you select the standing position, be sure to have a chair, counter, or piece of furniture for support should you need it.
2. Put the towel, bowl, and small items on the floor.
3. Start by using your right foot. Using only your toes, pick up the towel and put it into the bowl. This may not be easy at first but keep trying until you can pick up the towel on the first try.

4. Progress to picking up the smaller objects with your toes and putting them into the bowl. Once you have done this successfully, do the same exercise using the toes on your left foot.
5. Do as many repetitions as you are comfortable with. Try for 10.

Slowly ramp up:

Once you've mastered the process, you can use your toes to pick up other things on the floor. Try picking up an item with your toes and bringing it up to where you can reach it with your hands.

Caution:

If doing this exercise causes you pain, stop. Try bending your toes as if you were going to pick up the item. Gradually build the strength to pick up the item and put it into the bowl. If you still feel pain, skip this exercise and return to it when you have more strength and flexibility.

CHAPTER 11

INCREASING FLEXIBILITY

Increasing your flexibility is the second pillar of your exercise program. The many benefits of having adequate flexibility are discussed in Chapter 3. Flexibility is increased through stretching exercises. There are several types of stretches, but only two are recommended for seniors. These are dynamic and static stretches.

Dynamic Stretches

Dynamic stretches are movements designed to increase your heart rate and blood circulation. These exercises are excellent for warming up before your workout as they get your body moving and your blood flowing. The dynamic stretches in this book are recommended as warm-up exercises; thus, the number of repetitions and sets are less than if they were included in a full exercise routine. Add repetitions and sets if you are already in good physical condition and want to do more.

Static Stretches

Static stretches focus on stretching a single muscle or muscle group as far as it will go and then holding the stretch for several seconds. These exercises are great for reducing pain, achiness, and stiffness, and they increase flexibility. They are also a great way to cool down after a workout. They can help prevent contracting or cramping muscles and help with muscle recovery.

Follow these tips for safe stretching.

- Never push a stretch to the point of pain.
- Do not bounce at the end of a stretch to try and increase it.
- To increase the stretch, relax into it with a relaxed breath.
- Do not hold your breath while stretching. Breathe normally.
- Never stretch cold. Always ease into each stretch.

How often should I stretch?

Unless your doctor has advised you to limit your stretches, there is no limit to how often you can stretch. Stretch when you feel stressed or have been sitting for a while and need to move your body. Many stretches outlined in this book are "FIT FUN" exercises and can be done anytime during the day. Try doing a short stretching program in the morning to loosen your muscles and prepare you for the day. If you last exercised a while ago, start slow. Do some basic stretches several times weekly and work your way into a more frequent schedule.

A reminder:

Many of the exercises use standard terms and notations. For a refresher on these terms, refer to Chapter 9.

Dynamic Stretches – Warm- Up Exercises.

The following dynamic stretches provide a great warm-up. Do each exercise 5–10 times.

Start your warm-up with about five minutes of walking. You can start with a slow stroll and gradually increase your walking speed. Then follow with the following warm-up exercises:

March in Place

1. Place a chair in front of you for support, particularly if you have balance issues. Breathe normally.
2. Lift your knees as high as possible and march in place.
3. Get your legs moving and your heart rate up. March in place for 1 minute.
4. Then march forward for a minute and backward for a minute.

Squats

1. **Stand tall** with your feet shoulder-width apart. Your arms should be straight out in front of you, at shoulder height.
2. If you have balance issues, do these exercises with a wall behind you and a chair in front.
3. **Engage your core.** Breathe in.
4. Breathe out and push your hips back, bend your knees, and slowly lower your body into a squat. Do not let your knees cave in.
5. Keep a 45-degree arch on your upper back while keeping the lower back as straight as possible.
6. Push on your heels and slowly return to the starting position.
7. Always ensure you don't strain your knees.
8. Repeat for 5–10 repetitions.

Caution:

If the squat is too difficult for you, or you have a knee issue bothered by this exercise, start with semi-squats, that is, only go down part of the way. If this is still too difficult, sit on a chair with your feet on the floor rather than squat. Keep your chest out and knees out and push down through the floor to stand up. Then lower back into the chair.

Walking Lunge

1. **Stand tall** with your feet hip-width apart. Breathe in.
2. Breathe out as you step forward with your left leg, letting your right heel lift off the floor.
3. Bend your front (left) knee to lower your body until comfortable.
4. Allow your back (right) knee to bend until it hovers a few inches above the floor, but keep your weight pressed into your front heel.
5. **Engage your core** and lift your chest.
6. Pause, then breathe in, and press through your front (left) foot to bring your back (right) foot forward and return to standing. Continue alternating legs.
7. Repeat for 5–10 repetitions.

Caution:

If this is too difficult, or your knees bother you, only lower a few inches into the lunge rather than lowering until your front thigh a few inches from the floor.

Arm Circles

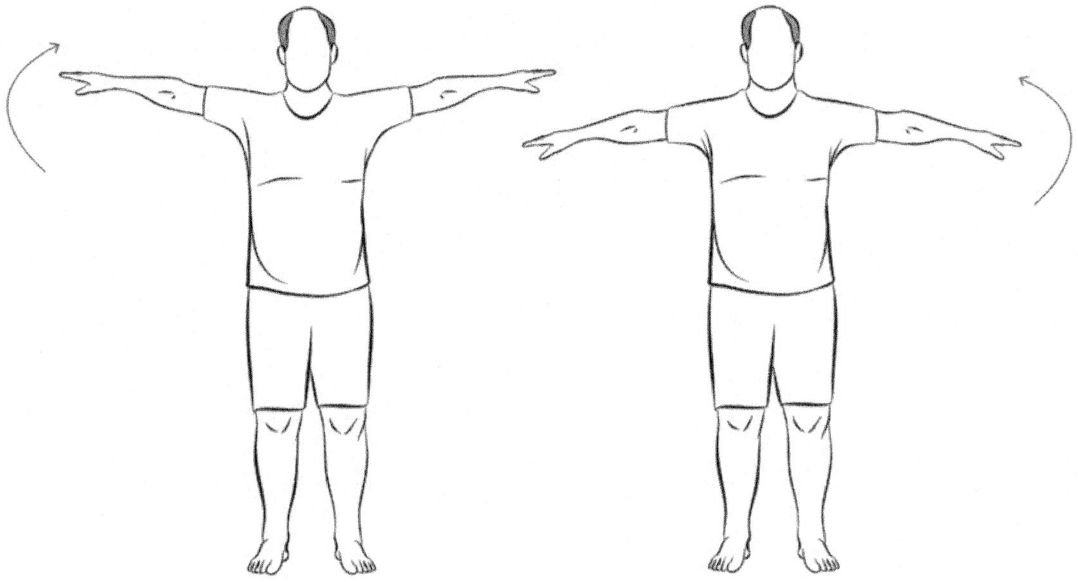

1. **Stand tall** with your feet hip-width apart. Breathe normally.
2. Extend your arms out to the sides at shoulder level with the palms facing down.
3. Swing your arms forward in a circular motion for 30 seconds. Swing them backward for 30 seconds. Be sure to keep your shoulders down.
4. Start with small circles for 30 seconds, then make your circles bigger for 30 seconds, then very wide for 30 seconds.
5. Repeat 5–10 times.

Shoulder Blade Squeeze

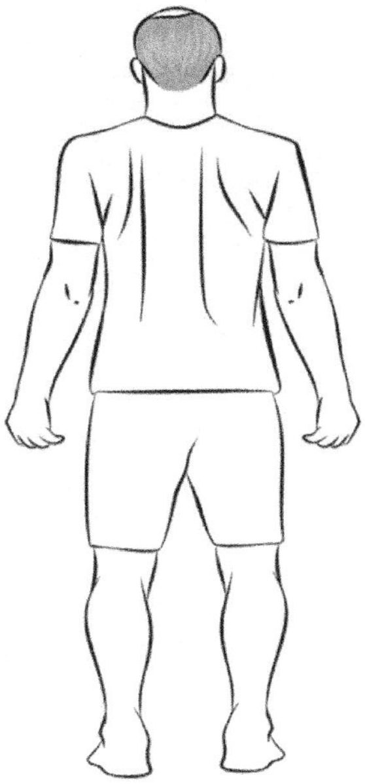

1. **Stand tall** with your feet hip-width apart. Breathe in.
2. Breathe out and pull your elbows back and down. Squeeze your shoulder blades together.
3. Imagine you are squeezing a lemon between your shoulder blades.
4. Hold the squeeze for 2–3 seconds, then release.
5. Repeat 5–10 times.

Punches

1. **Stand tall** and punch as if you are punching a punching bag. Breathe normally.
2. Use only up to 50% of your punching force to avoid injury.
3. Punch with your right fist, then your left fist.
4. Punch out each arm 5–10 times.
5. Then punch up toward the ceiling. Right arm, then left arm.
6. Repeat 5–10 times.

Static Stretches - Upper Body

Neck Flex

Position: Seated or Standing

Equipment Needed: None

Primary Area(s) Worked: Neck

1. **Sit tall** in a chair or **stand tall** with your shoulders back and down. Breathe normally.
2. Bring your chin down to your chest as far as you feel comfortable. You will feel a stretch in the back of the neck.
3. Place your hands on the back of your head and gently push your head forward.
4. Hold for 30 seconds.
5. Gradually build up to 3 sets.

Neck Extension

Position: Seated or Standing

Equipment Needed: None

Primary Area(s) Worked: Neck

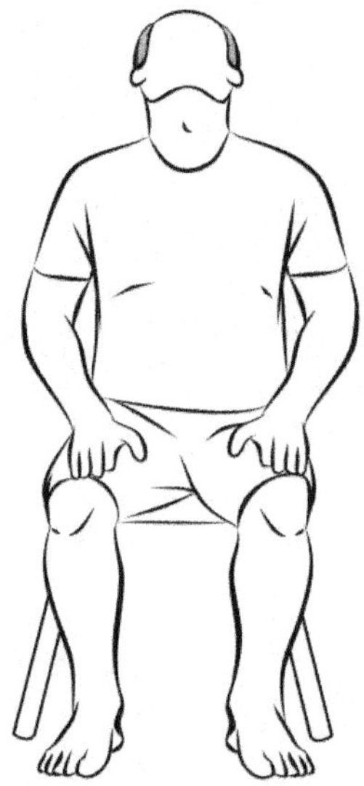

1. **Sit tall** in a chair or s**tand tall** with your shoulders back and down. Breathe normally.
2. Bring your head straight back as far as possible, looking up at the ceiling.
3. Hold for 30 seconds.
4. Gradually build up to 3 sets.

Neck Side Flexion

Position: Seated or Standing

Equipment Needed: None

Primary Area(s) Worked: Neck

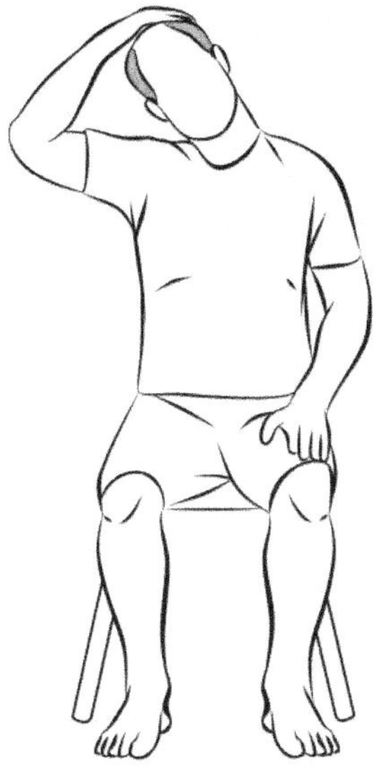

1. **Sit tall** in a chair or **stand tall** with your shoulders back and down. Breathe normally.
2. Bring your right ear down to your right shoulder. Go only as far as you feel comfortable.
3. Place your right hand on the left side of your head and gently pull your head to the right side.
4. Hold for 30 seconds.
5. Repeat on the left side.
6. Gradually build up to 3 sets.

Neck Rotation

Position: Seated or Standing

Equipment Needed: None

Primary Area(s) Worked: Neck

1. **Sit tall** in a chair or **stand tall** with your shoulders back and down. Breathe normally.
2. Look to the right side, twisting your neck as far as you feel comfortable.
3. Hold for 30 seconds.
4. Repeat on the left side.
5. Gradually build up to 3 sets.

Chin Tuck

Position: Seated or Standing

Equipment Needed: None

Primary Area(s) Worked: Neck

1. **Sit tall** or **stand tall** and look straight ahead. Your ears should be over your shoulders.
2. Place a finger on your chin. Breathe in.
3. Without moving your finger, breathe out and pull your chin and head back. Feel the stretch at the base of your head and the top of your neck.
4. Hold for 5–7 seconds.
5. Start with 10 repetitions.
6. Gradually build up to 5–7 sets done throughout the day.

Shoulder Stretch

Position: Seated or Standing

Equipment Needed: None

Primary Area(s) Worked: Shoulders

1. **Sit tall** in a chair or **stand tall** with your shoulders back and down. Breathe normally.
2. Place your right arm straight in front of your body and use your left wrist and forearm to pull the right arm toward your body.
3. Using your left arm, apply pressure to your right arm pulling it into a stretch.
4. Hold for 30 seconds.
5. Repeat on the left side.
6. Gradually build up to 3 sets.

Overhead Stretch

Position: Seated or Standing

Equipment Needed: None

Primary Area(s) Worked: Shoulders

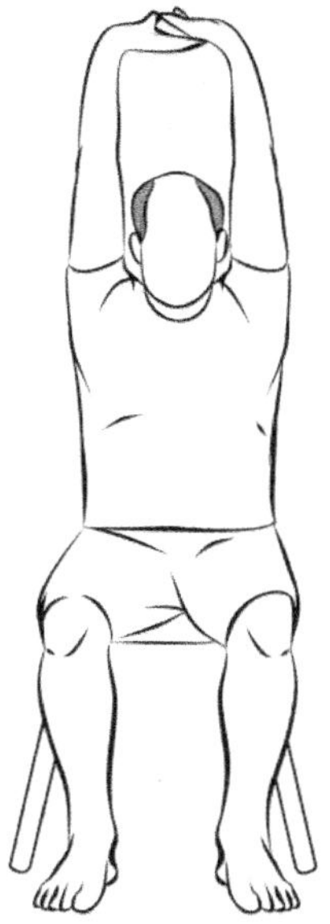

1. **Sit tall** in a chair or **stand tall** with your shoulders back and down. Breathe normally.
2. Interlace your fingers and bring your arms up above your head.
3. Your palms should face the ceiling. Push up as far as you can comfortably go.
4. Hold for 30 seconds.
5. Gradually build up to 3 sets.

Elbow Wrap Stretch

Position: Standing

Equipment Needed: None

Primary Area(s) Worked: Shoulders, Chest

1. **Stand tall** with both feet firmly planted on the floor. Breathe normally.
2. Bring your arms behind your back. Clasp each hand around the opposite elbow or forearm. Focus on squeezing your shoulder blades together.
3. Hold for 30 seconds.
4. Gradually build up to 3 sets.

Standing Chest Expansion

Position: Standing

Equipment Needed: Optional – Small Towel

Primary Area(s) Worked: Shoulders, Chest

1. **Stand tall** with your feet hip distance apart and a soft bend in your knees. Breathe normally.
2. Interweave your fingers together behind your lower back/hips. If this is too difficult, use a small towel to make up the distance.
3. Reach your hands away from your backside and open your chest up and out. The further you can draw your clasped hands away from your back, the better.
4. Hold for 30 seconds.
5. Gradually build up to 3 sets.

Shoulder Shrug

Position: Seated or Standing

Equipment Needed: None

Primary Area(s) Worked: Shoulders

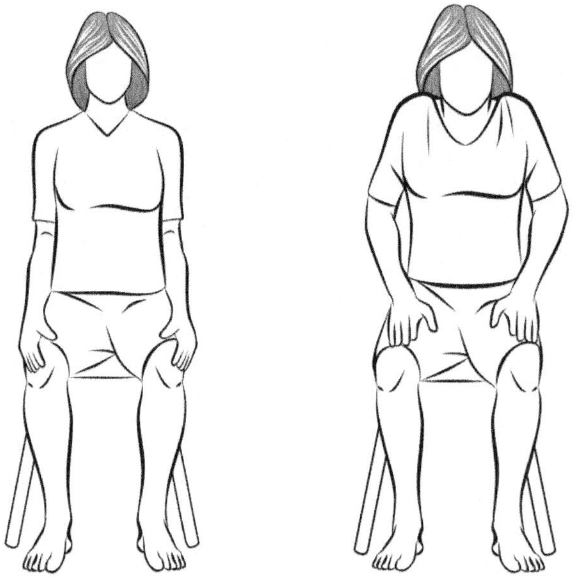

1. **Sit tall** in a chair or **stand tall** with your shoulders back and down.
2. Breathe in and slowly roll your shoulders up toward your ears.
3. Breathe out and bring your shoulders around and down.
4. Each complete exercise should take about 10 seconds. Perform this exercise 10 times.
5. Gradually build up to 3 sets.

Shoulder Pull

Position: Seated

Equipment Needed: None

Primary Area(s) Worked: Shoulders

1. **Sit tall** in a chair. Breathe normally.
2. Stretch your right arm and grab your outer left thigh.
3. Hold your head down, looking at your left thigh.
4. Slowly pull your upper body back, creating a stretch in your upper back, right shoulder, and arm.
5. Hold for 30 seconds.
6. Repeat on the left side.
7. Gradually build up to 3 sets.

Chest Expansion

Position: Seated or Standing

Equipment Needed: None

Primary Area(s) Worked: Chest

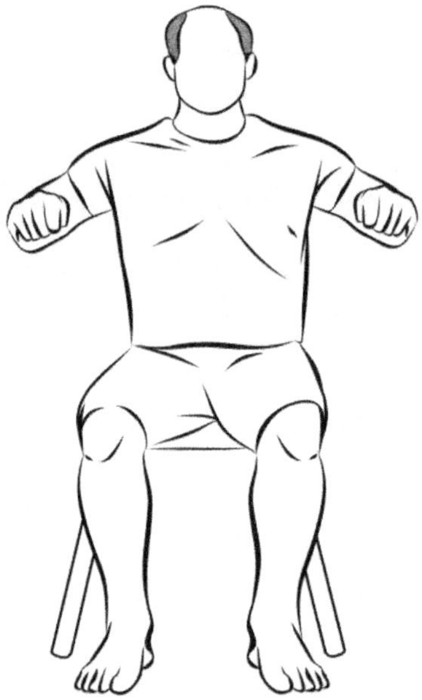

1. **Sit tall** in a chair or **stand tall** with your shoulders back and down. Breathe normally.
2. Put your arms out and pull your shoulders back as far as is comfortable and squeeze your shoulder blades together.
3. You should feel the stretch in your chest.
4. Hold for 30 seconds.
5. Gradually build up to 3 sets.

Upper Back Stretch

Position: Seated

Equipment Needed: None

Primary Area(s) Worked: Upper Back

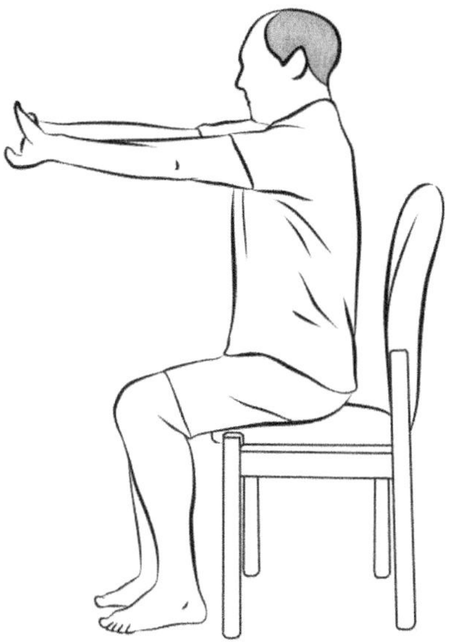

1. **Sit tall** in the middle of your chair with your shoulders back and down. Breathe normally.
2. Interlace your fingers and push your palms out away from you.
3. Bring your arms and interlaced fingers up and out about chest high.
4. Push your hands out as far as possible but feel comfortable. Be sure you keep your arms straight. You should be able to feel your shoulder blades stretch apart.
5. Hold for 30 seconds.
6. Gradually build up to 3 sets.

Upper Back Extension

Position: Seated

Equipment Needed: None

Primary Area(s) Worked: Upper Back

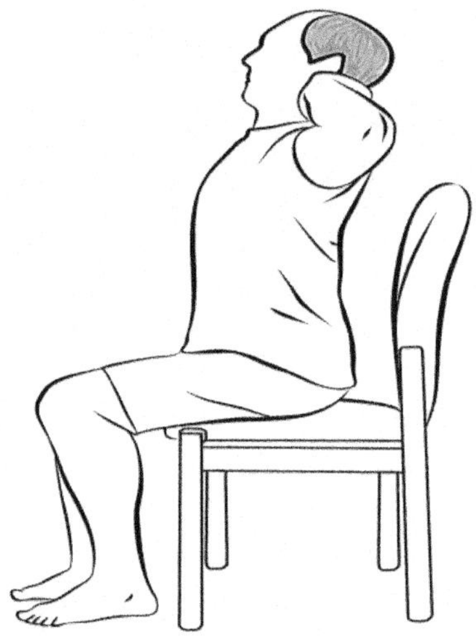

1. **Sit tall** in your chair with your shoulders back and down. Breathe normally.
2. Place your hands behind your head.
3. Maintain an upright position and extend your upper back over the chair.
4. Hold for 30 seconds.
5. Gradually build up to 3 sets.

Wrist and Forearm Flex /Down

Position: Seated, Standing, or Lying Down

Equipment Needed: None

Primary Area(s) Worked: Forearm and Wrist

1. **Sit tall** in a chair or **stand tall** with your shoulders back and down. Breathe normally.
2. Hold your right arm out straight in front of your body. Drop your wrist so that your palm and fingers are facing down.
3. Use your left hand and apply gentle pressure to the back of your right hand, just below the wrist; gently pull the hand and fingers toward the elbow. Be sure that your right arm remains straight throughout the stretch.
4. Hold for 30 seconds.
5. Repeat on the left side.
6. Gradually build up to 3 sets.

Flex Up

Position: Seated, Standing, or Lying Down

Equipment Needed: None

Primary Area(s) Worked: Forearm and Wrist

1. **Sit tall** in a chair or **stand tall** with your shoulders back and down. Breathe normally.
2. Hold your right arm out straight in front of your body. Your palms and fingers should be facing up.
3. Use your left hand, apply gentle pressure to the fingers on your right hand, and pull them back toward your elbow. Be sure that your right arm remains straight throughout the stretch.
4. Hold for 30 seconds.
5. Repeat on the left side.
6. Gradually build up to 3 sets.

Caution:

Skip this exercise if you have wrist pain (e.g., carpal tunnel syndrome) and this position aggravates the issue.

Squeeze the Ball

Position: Seated, Standing, or Lying Down

Equipment Needed: Tennis Balls

Primary Area(s) Worked: Wrists, Elbows, Fingers

1. **Sit tall** in a chair, **engage your core,** pull your shoulders back, and push your chest out.
2. Hold a tennis ball in each hand. Your arms should be up, with hands about ear height. If you can't raise your arms, keep them on your lap and squeeze the balls. Breathe in.
3. Breathe out and slowly squeeze the balls. Breathe in and release.
4. Make sure you are using all your fingers.
5. Start with 10 repetitions on both hands.
6. Gradually build up to 3 sets.

Caution:

If your hands are weak, slowly squeeze as much as possible without causing pain.

Finger Spread

Position: Seated, Standing, or Lying Down

Equipment Needed: None

Primary Area(s) Worked: Fingers

This is a 2-part exercise:

Part 1

1. **Sit tall** in a chair, shoulders back, chest out, and **engage your core.**
2. Place the index and middle finger of your left hand between your index and middle finger on your right hand and spread the fingers of your right hand.

3. Repeat between the 3rd and 4th fingers on the right hand, then the 4th and 5th fingers, and then the thumb and index fingers on the right hand.
4. Breathe normally and hold each stretch for 5 seconds.
5. Perform the same stretch using the right hand to stretch the fingers of the left hand.
6. Start with 10 repetitions on both hands.
7. Gradually build up to 3 sets.

Part 2

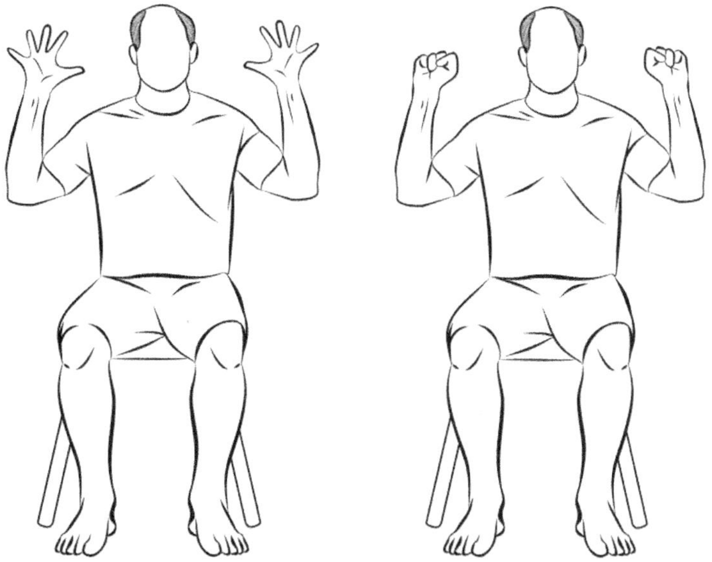

1. Hold both hands up and open as wide as possible for 5 seconds.
2. Close your hands, making a fist. Hold for 5 seconds. Breathe normally and repeat.
3. Start with 10 repetitions on both hands.
4. Gradually build up to 3 sets.

Thumb Press

Position: Seated, Standing, or Lying Down

Equipment needed: None

Primary Area(s) Worked: Fingers

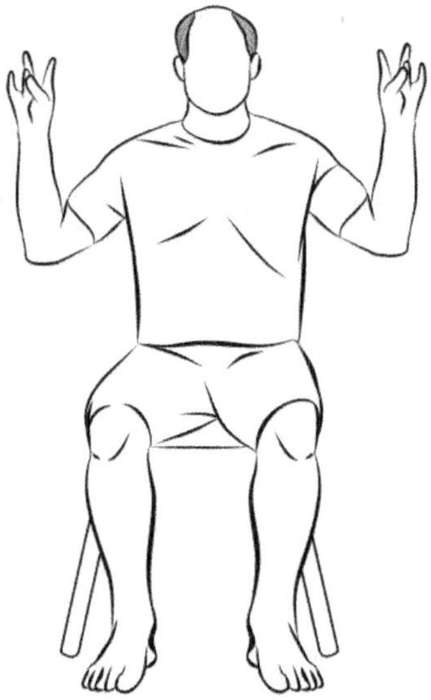

1. **Sit tall** in a chair, **engage your core**, shoulders back, and chest out. Breathe normally.
2. Hold both hands up and open as wide as you can.
3. Touch your thumbs to your index finger. Open your hand wide.
4. Continue the process, touching your thumb to your middle finger and opening the hand wide.
5. Continue the process for each finger.
6. Start with 10 repetitions on both hands. Gradually build up to 3 sets.

Static Stretches – Lower Body

Lower Back Extension

Position: Seated

Equipment Needed: None

Primary Area(s) Worked: Lower Back

1. **Sit tall** in the middle of your chair with your shoulders back and down.
2. Place your hands on the small of your back with your palms supporting your lower back.
3. Slowly lean your lower back into your hands. Feel the stretch in your lower back.
4. Breathe Normally
5. Hold for 30 seconds.
6. Gradually build up to 3 sets.

Caution:

Skip this exercise if you have lower back pain, and this position aggravates the issue.

Lower Back Side Flex

Position: Seated

Equipment Needed: None

Primary Area(s) Worked: Lower Back

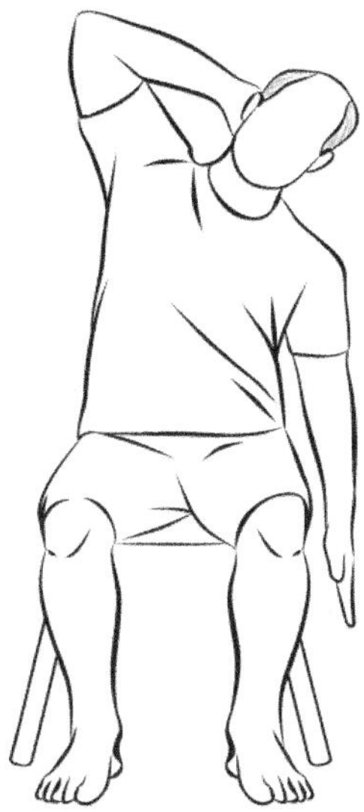

1. **Sit tall** in the middle of your chair with your shoulders back and down. Breathe normally.
2. Place your left hand behind your head. Keep your back straight and drop your right arm straight beside you. Slowly lean down to the right side with the straight arm until you can feel a stretch on the opposite side. Be careful not to twist your spine or waist.
3. Hold for 30 seconds.
4. Repeat on the left side.
5. Gradually build up to 3 sets.

Hamstring Stretch

Position: Lying Down

Equipment needed: None

Primary Area(s) Worked: Hamstrings

1. Lie down on your bed or the floor. Breathe normally.
2. Raise your right leg and hold it as straight as possible but still be comfortable. You should feel the stretch in your hamstring muscles.
3. Hold for 30 seconds and then return the leg to the floor/ bed.
4. Repeat on the left side.
5. Gradually build up to 3 sets.

Thigh Pull Stretch

Position: Lying down

Equipment needed: None

Primary Area(s) Worked: Thighs, Upper Leg

1. Lie down on your bed or the floor. Breathe normally.
2. Bend both knees and bring your right knee to your chest.
3. Place your hands behind your right thigh and pull your leg as close to you as possible.
4. Hold for 30 seconds.
5. Repeat on the left side.
6. Gradually build up to 3 sets.

Figure Four Stretch

Position: Lying down

Equipment needed: None

Primary Area(s) Worked: Upper Leg, Hips

1. Lie down on your bed or the floor. Breathe normally.
2. Bring both knees to your chest.
3. Place your left knee over your right knee.
4. Hold the back of your right thigh with both hands and pull toward you to gently stretch the hips.
5. Use your left forearm to gently push your left thigh down.
6. The position of your legs and arms should almost resemble a figure four.
7. Hold for 30 seconds.
8. Repeat on the left side.
9. Gradually build up to 3 sets.

Seated Hamstring

Position: Seated

Equipment Needed: None

Primary Area(s) Worked: Hamstrings

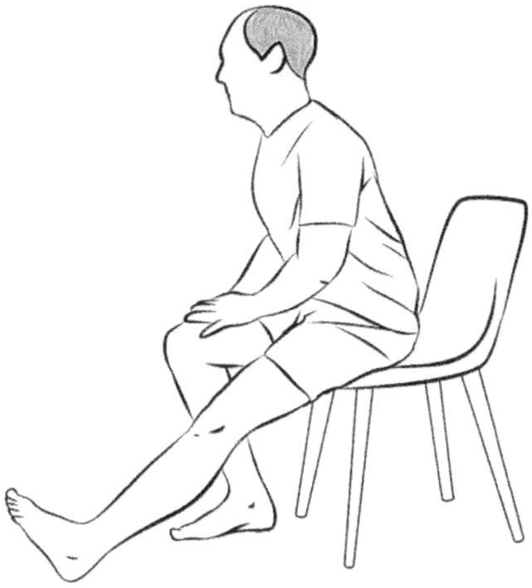

1. **Sit tall** at the front of your chair.
2. Put both hands on your left knee. Breathe normally.
3. Straighten your right leg in front of you. Point your toes toward the ceiling.
4. Keep your back straight and lean over your extended right leg.
5. Hold for 30 seconds.
6. Repeat on the left side.
7. Gradually build up to 3 sets.

Standing Quad Stretch

Position: Standing

Equipment needed: None

Primary Area(s) Worked: Quads

1. **Stand tall** next to a chair. Hold onto the chair with one arm. Breathe normally.
2. Bring your right leg up behind you. Hold onto your foot with your right hand.
3. Keep your back straight and your knees as close together as possible.
4. Hold for 30 seconds.
5. Repeat on the left side.
6. Gradually build up to 3 sets.

Seated Glute Stretch

Position: Seated

Equipment needed: None

Primary Area(s) Worked: Glutes

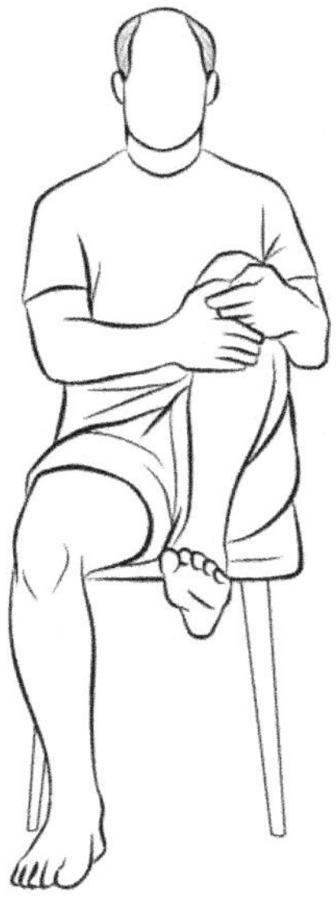

1. **Sit tall** at the front of your chair. Breathe Normally.
2. Lift your right leg up and, bending at the knee, bring it to your chest. Hug your knee.
3. Hold for 30 seconds.
4. Repeat on the left side.
5. Gradually build up to 3 sets.

Seated Hip Stretch

Position: Seated

Equipment Needed: None

Primary Area(s) Worked: Hips

1. **Sit tall** at the front of your chair. Breathe Normally.
2. Stretch your right leg out to the side. Keep the toes on your right foot firmly on the ground and facing forward.
3. Your left foot should be on the ground and face forward.
4. Keeping your back straight, lean slightly forward. You should feel a stretch in your right inner thigh.
5. Hold for 30 seconds.
6. Repeat on the left side.
7. Gradually build up to 3 sets.

Standing Hip Stretch

Position: Standing

Equipment Needed: None

Primary Area(s) Worked: Hips and Upper Leg

1. **Stand tall.** Move each leg out to the side. Face your toes outward. Breathe normally.
2. Keep a chair in front of you when performing this exercise.
3. Bend your right knee and shift your weight to the right side. You should feel the stretch in your right inner thigh.
4. Hold for 30 seconds.
5. Repeat on the left side.
6. Gradually build up to 3 sets.

Standing Calf Stretch

Position: Standing

Equipment Needed: None

Primary Area(s) Worked: Calf, Back of Leg

1. **Stand tall,** holding onto your chair with both hands. Breathe normally.
2. Bring your right foot back. Make sure your toes are facing forward.
3. Bend your left knee forward toward the chair so that you feel a stretch in your right calf. Make sure both heels are on the floor.
4. Hold for 30 seconds.
5. Repeat on the left side.
6. Gradually build up to 3 sets

CHAPTER 12

IMPROVING BALANCE

Improved balance is the focus of the third pillar of our exercise program.

Good balance comes from a strong and flexible body. As you do the exercises presented in Chapters 10 and 11, you will build strength and flexibility in your legs, ankles, abdomen, hips, spine, core, and upper body. You also improve your balance as you build strength and flexibility in these body areas.

In addition, the following targeted exercises improve your balance quickly as they strengthen multiple areas of your body with each movement. You can do these as a standalone sequence or combined with other exercises from this book.

How often should I do targeted balance exercises?

You can do these daily if you have balance issues. More on this in Chapter 14.

A reminder:

Many of the exercises use standard terms and notations. For a refresher on these terms, refer to Chapter 9.

Balance Exercises

Three-Way Toe Tap

Position: Standing

Equipment needed: Optional Folded Towel

Primary Area(s) Worked: Abdomen, Hips

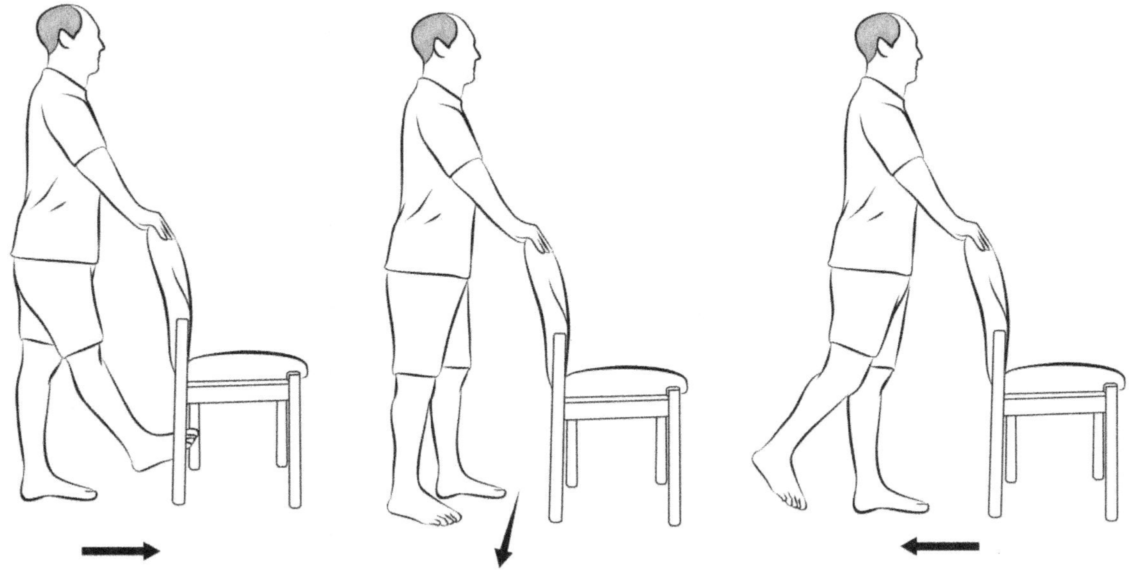

1. Use the back of a sturdy chair or countertop for support.
2. **Stand tall** behind the chair with your legs hip-width apart. Breathe normally.
3. Keep your left leg straight. Extend your right foot out, point it in front of you at the 12 o'clock position, and tap the floor. Extend your right foot to the side of you at the 3 o'clock position and tap the floor. Extend your right foot behind you at the 6 o'clock position and tap the floor. Breathe normally.

4. Repeat this sequence 10 times using your right leg.
5. Then repeat the exercise using your left leg. With your right foot straight, point your left foot in front of you at 12 o'clock, and tap the floor. Extend your left leg to the side of you at the 9 o'clock position and tap the floor. Extend your left foot behind you at the 6 o'clock position and tap the floor.
6. Repeat this sequence 10 times using your left leg.
7. Start with 10 repetitions. Gradually build up to 3 sets or 30 repetitions.

Slowly ramp up:

Stand on a folded towel so that your straight leg is on a slightly raised platform. Perform the same exercise using the towel to elevate your straight leg.

Caution:

If doing this exercise causes you pain, stop. Try adjusting your stance or not extending your leg as far out. If you still feel pain, skip this exercise and return to it when you have more strength and flexibility.

Side-to-Side

Position: Standing

Equipment needed: None

Primary Area(s) Worked: Abdomen, Hip, Glutes, Quads, Lower Leg (Calves and Shin)

1. If you are feeling unsteady, do this exercise near a countertop or sturdy chair for support.
2. Take a wide stance to start. Place your arms at your waist. If you feel unsteady, keep one or both hands lightly on your support item. Breathe in.
3. With a gently rocking motion, transfer your weight to the right leg. Breathe out and bend your right knee while keeping your left leg straightened out.
4. Breathe in, and slowly transfer your weight back to the center.

5. With a gently rocking motion, transfer your weight to the left leg. Breathe out as you bend your left knee while keeping your right leg straightened out.
6. This exercise takes on a gentle see-saw movement.
7. One repletion is a movement to each side and back to center. Start with 10 repetitions. Gradually build up to 3 sets or 30 repetitions.

Slowly ramp up:

When you are confident with your balance and ability to do this exercise, practice this on your walks. Turn sideways and sidestep for 10 steps. Turn the other way and sidestep for 10 steps. Repeat as many repetitions as you are comfortable with.

Caution:

If doing this exercise causes you pain, stop. Adjust your position, make your stance less wide, or do not bend your knee as deep. If you still feel pain, skip this exercise, and return to it when you have more strength and flexibility.

Sit to Stand

Position: Standing

Equipment needed: Chair

Primary Area(s) Worked: Abdomen, Lower Back, Glutes, Quads, Hamstrings

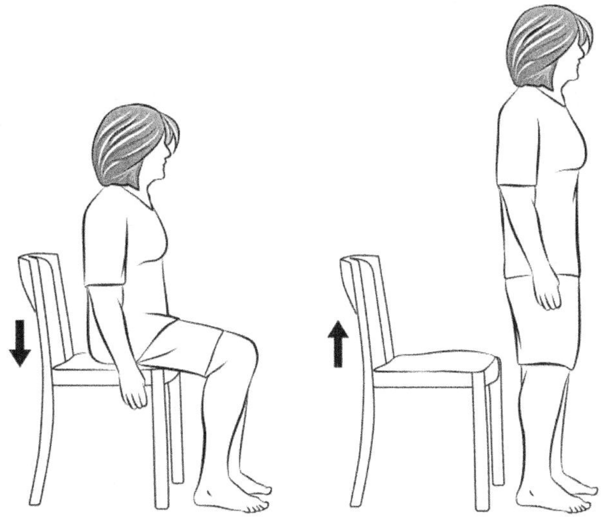

1. You will need a sturdy chair that will not move to do this exercise. If your balance is not good, do this exercise close to a countertop or large furniture for support.
2. **Sit tall** in the chair with your feet about hip-width apart. Breathe in.
3. Breathe out and slowly stand up. Press through your heels and squeeze your glutes as you stand up. Using the muscles in your heels and legs, not your torso, is essential.
4. Keep standing for about 10 seconds to get your balance.

5. Breathe in and slowly sit back in the chair. Keep your weight mainly on your heels. Again, use the muscles in your heels and legs, not your torso.
6. One repetition is the completion of the standing/sitting sequence.
7. Start with 10 repetitions. Gradually build up to 3 sets or 30 repetitions.

Slowly ramp up:

Instead of sitting back fully into the chair, go down into a sitting position but stop a few inches from the chair seat. Hold about 10 seconds and then go back to the standing position.

Caution:

If doing this exercise causes you pain, stop. Try using your hands or arms to steady yourself as you sit and stand up. If you still feel pain, skip this exercise and return to it when you have more strength and flexibility.

Wall Press

Position: Standing

Equipment needed: None

Primary Area(s) Worked: Shoulders, Chest, Triceps, Abdomen, Glutes, Quads, and Calves

1. Find a sturdy wall in your home.
2. Stand with your feet slightly apart, about an arm's distance from the wall.
3. Put both palms on the wall, with your wrists in line with your shoulders. Point your fingers toward the ceiling.
4. **Engage your core.** Slightly pinch your shoulder blades back and down as if you Are holding a can between your shoulders. Breathe in.

5. Breathe out and bend your elbows straight back until your forehead touches the wall.
6. Breathe in as you slowly press away from the wall and back to a standing position.
7. Start with 10 repetitions. Gradually build up to 3 sets or 30 repetitions.

Slowly ramp up:

Try performing the same sequence but tilt forward on your toes (as if you are on your tiptoes) and move your arms lower on the wall.

Caution:

If doing this exercise causes you pain, stop. Step closer to the wall and try the exercise again. If you still feel pain, skip this exercise and return to it when you have more strength and flexibility.

Stand on One Foot

Position: Standing

Equipment Needed: None

Primary Area(s) Worked: Abdominals, Quads, Hamstrings, Calves, Ankles

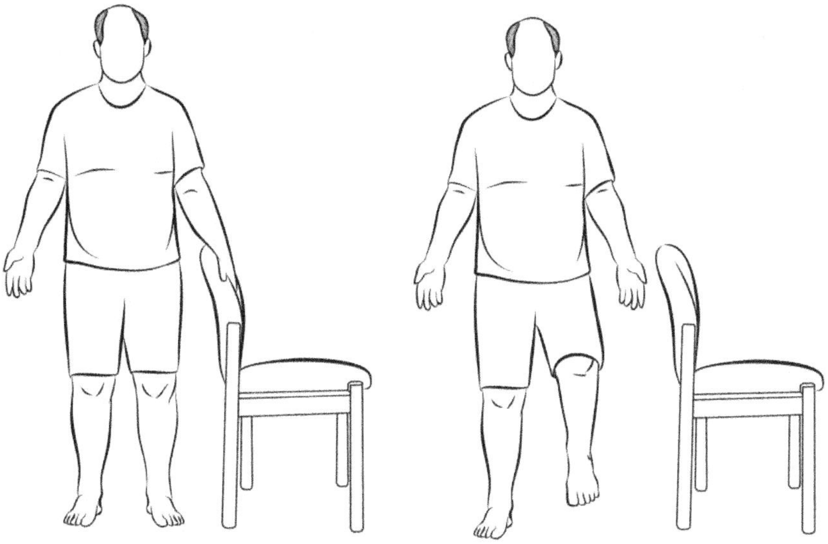

1. Use the back of a sturdy chair or countertop to provide support.
2. **Stand tall** with feet about hip-width apart. Hold onto the back of the chair if needed for balance. Breathe normally.
3. Stand on your left leg and lift your right leg off the floor. Continue to stand tall without putting too much weight on the standing leg. Hold for 10 seconds, then lower your foot.
4. Switch legs. Stand on your right leg and lift your left leg off the floor. Hold for 10 seconds. Continue to stand tall without putting too much weight on the standing leg. Hold for 10 seconds.

5. Start with 10 repetitions. Gradually build up to 3 sets or 30 repetitions.
6. Exercise without holding onto the chair as your confidence and balance increase.

Slowly ramp up:

Instead of lifting your leg and holding it up, begin by standing on the right leg and lifting your left leg up until it is about knee height. Touch your left foot to your right leg and hold for 10 seconds. Repeat by standing on your left leg and lifting your right leg up until it is about knee height. Touch your right foot to your left leg and hold for 10 seconds.

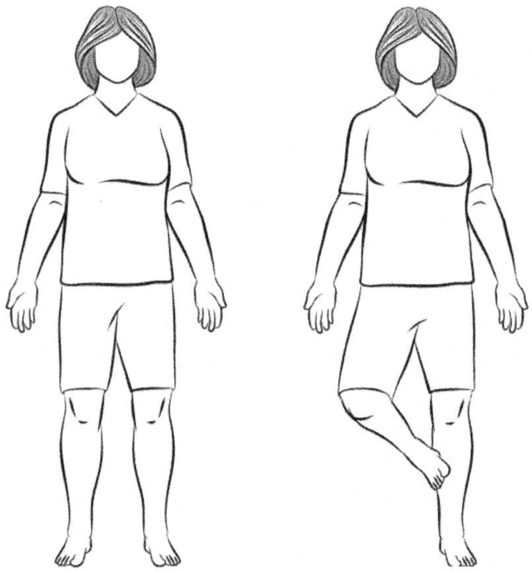

Caution:

If doing this exercise causes you pain, stop. Be sure you are using the chair for support. Try lowering the level that you lift your leg and try again. If you still feel pain, skip this exercise and return to it when you have more strength and flexibility.

Heel Raises

Position: Standing

Equipment Needed: Optional: Small Folded Towel

Primary Area(s) Worked: Calves, Ankles, Feet

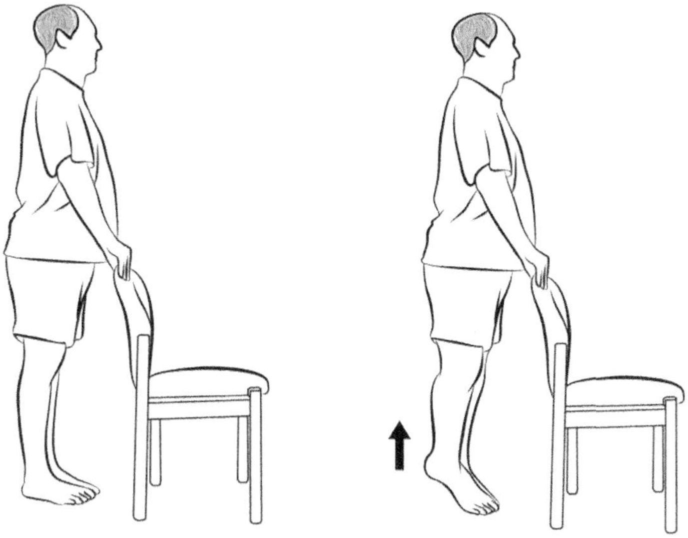

1. Use the back of a sturdy chair or countertop for support.
2. Stand tall with feet about hip-width apart. Hold onto the back of the chair or countertop if your balance is not good. Breathe normally.
3. Slowly lift your heels off the ground so that your body lifts upward onto the balls of your feet and the heels are elevated.
4. Go as high as you can comfortably and pause at the top for 1–3 seconds.
5. Slowly lower your heels back down.
6. Start with 10 repetitions. Gradually build up to 3 sets or 30 repetitions.

Slowly ramp up:

When you are comfortable with your balance, discontinue using the chair for support. You can also fold up a small towel and place it under the balls of your feet so that when you lift your heels, the front part of your feet will be elevated.

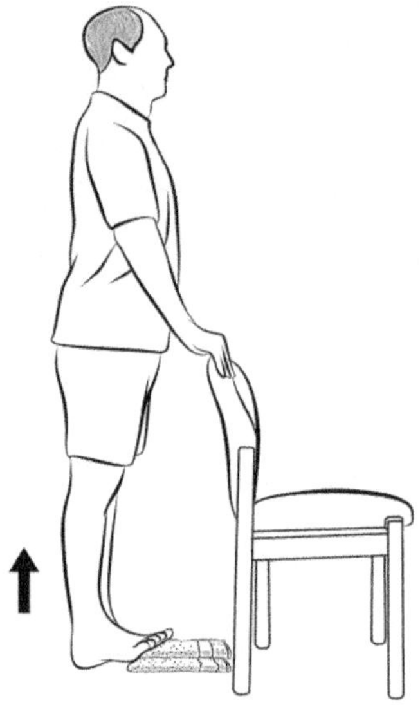

Caution:

If doing this exercise causes you pain, stop. Be sure you are using the chair for support. Try lowering the level as you lift your heels off the ground and try again. If you still feel pain, skip this exercise and return to it when you have more strength and flexibility.

Toe Raises

Position: Seated

Equipment Needed: None

Primary Area(s) Worked: Calves, Ankles, Feet

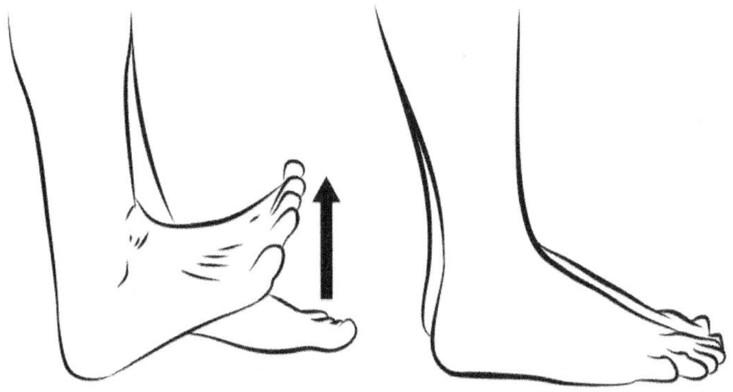

1. **Sit tall** in a chair with your feet on the floor. Place your hands on your thighs. Breathe normally.
2. Slowly raise your toes off the ground. Ensure you do not lean over but continue to sit upright.
3. Hold for 10 seconds, then lower your toes.
4. Repeat 10 times. Gradually build up to 3 sets or 30 repetitions.

Slowly ramp up:

Alternate between raising your toes and then your heels.

Caution:

If doing this exercise causes you pain, stop. If your calf or ankle muscles start to burn, go lower and rest between toe raises. If you still feel pain, skip this exercise and return to it when you have more strength and flexibility.

CHAPTER 13

BUILDING ENDURANCE

Building endurance is the fourth pillar of your exercise program.

Endurance, or aerobic exercises, involve active movements that increase your breathing and heart rate. Aerobic exercise increases oxygen consumption and, when done consistently, can increase your stamina and endurance.

Unless you are very fit, many types of aerobic exercises that you may have done when you were younger, like jumping rope, long-distance running, jogging, or participating in very active aerobic exercise classes, may not be safe for you to do as you age.

The following exercises are great ways for seniors to increase their endurance and stability.

Cycling

Cycling can be an excellent aerobic exercise, especially if you have a physically limiting condition like the ones discussed earlier in this book. Cycling can be done inside with a stationary bike or outside, where we can enjoy nature. Cycling reduces stress and lowers cholesterol while improving testosterone levels in men. Cycling also improves T-cell production and immunity.

Swimming

If you have knee problems, swimming is an excellent aerobic exercise. It provides a whole-body workout that is gentle on the knees and joints. The water offers a mild form of resistance. Check your local community or private swim school facilities for a pool. Many offer water exercise classes designed for seniors. If a water aerobics class is unavailable, one of the best exercises is walking back and forth in the pool. Walking in the pool for 15–30 minutes can significantly build your endurance and muscle strength.

Dancing

If you have a partner who loves to dance, you can get your aerobic exercise in while spending a delightful evening on the dance floor. Check out your local community recreational center if you need a partner. Many centers offer line dancing and other opportunities to kick up your heels, with or without a partner. If these options don't work, play music and dance around your house as you do housework or normal daily activities. The objective is to get off the sofa and move those legs.

Walking

Walking is one of the best ways to move your body, increase your heart rate, and build endurance. It's always fun to connect with a friend as you go for a walk together. You can enjoy the beautiful outdoors and some social time while also getting some exercise. If the weather is not good, there are also options to walk indoors. Many people walk through an indoor shopping mall before it opens to the public. Be creative and look for ways to get your body moving.

How much aerobic exercise should we get?

The CDC recommends that adults 65 and older get at least 150 minutes of moderate-intensity aerobic activity weekly.

You are doing "moderate-intensity" activity if you are walking, cycling, swimming, etc., and breathing hard, but you can still carry on a conversation. You are doing vigorous-intensity activities if you exercise hard enough to only say a few words before taking a breath.

Take it slow if you last exercised a while ago or are recovering from a health issue or physical injury. There is no need to go for the gold medal immediately. Ease your way into it. Give your body adequate rest in between exercise sessions. It takes time to build endurance in your heart and muscles, so start with what you can handle and add a few minutes to each workout to work your way up gradually.

Ramping Up

You can ramp up once you are comfortable with your stamina. There are several good ways to do this:

- Activity Trackers – Investing in an activity tracker or phone app to track your endurance is an easy and fun way to build up your endurance. These are inexpensive and can be purchased on Amazon or at your local retailer. Many seniors track the number of steps they take each day. If this is your goal, start based on where you are physically now. Three thousand steps a day may be a good starting goal if you haven't walked for a while. Your goal may be 6,000 to 10,000 steps if you are more active. The number of steps is not the primary goal. The main objective is to use this tool as a fun way to help you gradually increase your movement and thereby slowly build your stamina and endurance.
- Weights - carry weights as you walk or wear a weighted vest while doing endurance exercises.

Interval Training – Interval workouts alternate periods of high-intensity exercise with low-intensity recovery periods. Research has shown that interval training increases endurance and helps with weight loss. So, when walking, cycling, swimming, or walking in the pool, go as fast as you can for 1–2 minutes, then drop back into a slower, more relaxed pace for 5 minutes. Repeat this for the duration of your exercise period. Adding interval training to your routine can be challenging, so go slowly and allow your body time to adjust. You are not in a race, so you can go at your own pace, steadily building as you can.

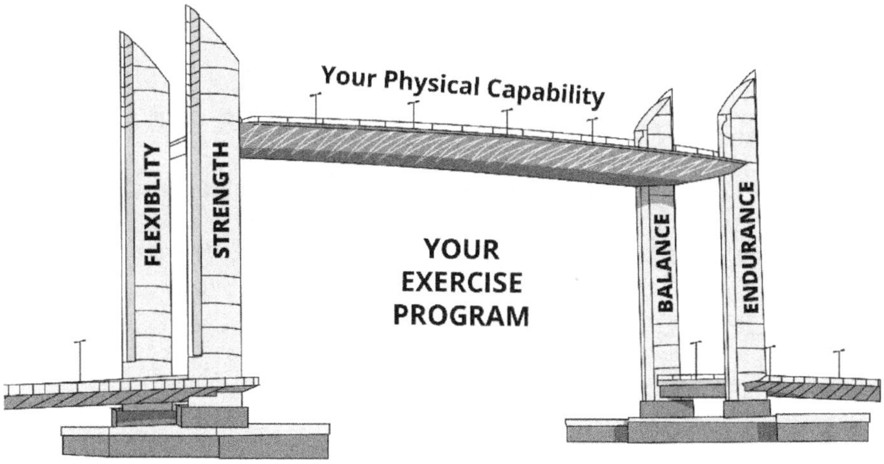

CHAPTER 14

PULLING IT ALL TOGETHER

This book provides the information you need to develop and implement an exercise program that works for you. The key phrase here is "that works for you." With this objective in mind, there are two programs you can choose from.

Create Your Own Program

This program is excellent if you have specific objectives that you want to focus on or if you like to chart your own path. You may feel stiff and want to focus on flexibility initially. Your balance may be a little off, and you want to work on improving this first. Your legs may be weak, and you want to add additional lower-body strength-building exercises to your program. If you like the flexibility to choose your path, the "Create Your Own Program" is best for you.

Four Week Ageless Agility Program

This program is excellent if you want a program that is mapped out for you, a program that focuses on the four pillars of exercise and provides a roadmap of what exercises to do daily to achieve results. If you want to follow a defined exercise schedule daily, the "Four Week Ageless Agility" program is for you.

Regardless of what program you decide to follow, remember that you know your body best, and you may need to tailor these exercises to your needs. Follow the earlier guidelines about ramping the exercise up or down based on your physical condition. Remember, you are in control.

Be sure to do warm-up exercises before you begin either of these programs. The warm-up exercises are covered in Chapter 11 under Dynamic Stretches. Appendix I includes a summary of these stretches.

Create Your Own Exercise Program

Let's start by reviewing the four pillars of a good exercise plan. You can choose from these as you feel would best meet your needs and objectives. A summary list of all the exercises is included in Appendix II.

Strength Building

The CDC recommends that adults strive to do exercises that strengthen all the major muscle groups at least two days a week. It is essential to allow your body to rest for at least one day after each strength training routine. Resting for two days is better, and you may need more than this to allow your joints and muscles to heal and prevent fatigue.

If you are a beginner, start with strength-building exercises two times a week. Start with one set of the recommended repetitions and gradually increase the number of sets.

If you have been exercising for a while, try to do all the sets recommended and consider increasing your strength-building exercises to three times per week.

If you want to kick it up a notch, focus on your upper body two days a week and your lower body two days a week. Just allow at least one day of rest between working a muscle group. For example, Monday and Wednesday work your upper body, and Tuesday and Thursday work your lower body and core. If you want to focus on building strength in your upper or lower body, add more of these targeted exercises into your routine.

Flexibility – Stretches

Stretching is always beneficial. At a minimum, the CDC recommends stretching exercises at least 2–3 days a week. If you are feeling stiff or want to increase your flexibility, perform these exercises 4–5 days a week. Consider creating a morning stretch routine to help get your day off to a great start.

Balance Exercises

You can do targeted balance exercises daily, but at a minimum, you should do exercises to improve your balance at least twice a week. If you have balance issues, add these exercises to your weekly plan more often.

Endurance Building Exercises

The CDC recommends that seniors do 150 minutes per week of walking, swimming, biking, etc. Experiment with different ways to do this. Try for 30 minutes five days a week or about 20 minutes every seven days. If this is difficult for you, break it up throughout the day, such as walking for 15 minutes after breakfast and 15 minutes after dinner. If you want to ramp up, increase the time or number of steps you take and the speed you walk, swim, bike, etc.

Change It Up

We are a creature of habit, and it is easy to do the same thing every day and every week. The problem is that our body becomes comfortable, and you may get less impact from your workout. When you start your exercise program, your body needs to adapt to cope with the stress you put on it. After a while, it doesn't need any more changes and is not making the adaptations that challenge the muscle group. Sports physical therapists use "Periodization" to describe a systematic approach for varying exercise routines for safety and to achieve maximum results. They typically use one of the following:

- Linear periodization - Gradually increase the number of repetitions and weights over a period of time. For example, start with lighter weights and more repetitions and progressively build to heavier weights and fewer repetitions.
- Undulating periodization - Varies the number of repetitions and intensity (amount of weight) with each workout.
- Block periodization - Focuses on one goal at a time. For example, focus on flexibility exercises for a month, strength-building exercises for a month, and endurance-building exercises for a month.

Use or vary one of these methods to create an approach that works for you.

FIT FUN Exercises

If you are short on time or unable to follow a set routine, see how many of these fun, easy exercises you can fit into your day. Turn it into a game and challenge yourself to do more each day. With FIT FUN exercises, staying fit becomes almost effortless.

Four Week Ageless Agility Exercise Program

The Four Week Ageless Agility Program provides a defined exercise routine for each day of the four weeks. It is designed to build continuous muscle growth, improve balance, improve endurance, and increase flexibility. It incorporates each type of periodization during the four weeks.

There are two plans:

Beginner's Four-Week Plan

The four-week beginner routine includes two strength days and a balance and flexibility day. The other days have lower-intensity flexibility, balance, endurance, and FIT FUN exercises. This mix allows you to perform some daily physical activity while giving your muscles enough time to recover. The types of exercises and intensity vary daily and weekly, so variety is built into the program.

Intermediate Four-Week Plan

The intermediate Program contains everything the beginner plan includes regarding the types of exercises and the approach for varying exercises throughout the weeks. The primary differences are in the intensity of the exercises and the number of strength and endurance routines performed during the week. This Program includes three strength workouts per week (compared to two strength days in the beginner program). The number of endurance exercises and the duration of these exercises also increase. The four-week intermediate routine provides more visible impacts on strength, endurance, flexibility, and balance. This plan is a road map for those seniors who are already physically fit.

The Mind-Muscle Connection

It is recommended that everyone complete the beginner program at least once before jumping into the intermediate exercise program. Starting with the beginner program will ensure maximum safety and better mind-muscle connection.

When an exercise is new, your muscle fibers take time to overcome a new, challenging activity. Your brain also needs time to identify the movements involved in this exercise and coordinate your muscle fibers with proper neural responses. When you do the beginner exercise program, you learn new moves, even if you have substantial experience in fitness. You keep the intensity manageable in the beginner program and learn the new exercise variations with maximum impact by building your mind-muscle connection. Once you are trained enough in the beginner program, you will use your expertise and challenge yourself more in the intermediate program.

Because all exercises of the intermediate program have been mastered in the beginner routine, you will develop increased strength by only focusing on the intensity. Also, you will be more agile and flexible and have better stamina plus balance. That way, you will reap the maximum benefits of increased intensity.

Generally, if you have less than six months of recent exercise experience, use the beginner program twice before jumping into the intermediate program. If you have six or more months of recent experience in exercise as an active senior, complete the beginner program once only and move to the intermediate program.

The “Four Week Ageless Agility” exercise plans are included in Appendix III.

A Caution About Overexercising

Throughout this book, I have been touting the many proven benefits of a good exercise program and encouraging you to start your program. But in your zeal to get started, you must also be sure you don't overdo it. Yes, you can indeed overexercise; this may not be the norm for most people. Still, it can happen, particularly if you love to immediately "go for the gold" with everything you do.

The term "overexercise" means to do excessive physical activity to the point where you may harm your health. Our body's ability to recover and heal decreases as we age. Overdoing it could result in sprains, injuries, or strains on the body systems. Excessive overexercise can also have more severe consequences and affect heart function, bone mass, and testosterone levels in men. One of the most important reasons not to overdo it is the likely effect it will have on your motivation to continue. If you burn out in the first couple of weeks, are unusually sore, or worst case, injure yourself, it is unlikely that you will continue over the long haul.

So, if you start feeling overly tired for no other reason, such as late nights or illness, or you are feeling excessively sore after adequate rest or not sleeping, then you may be overexercising.

If that is the case, adjust your program.

- Set realistic goals - Start by setting a workout goal that is realistic and reasonable for you.
- Focus on consistency - Focus on being consistent and gradually increasing your workout's intensity and length rather than pushing yourself too hard too soon.
- Schedule additional rest days – Allow your body more time to rest and restore between workout sessions.
- Vary your activities - Changing up your exercise routine can help with boredom and reduce the risk of overexercising. Vary your activities - Changing up your exercise routine can help with boredom and reduce the risk of overexercising.
- Keep yourself hydrated – Drink water before, during, and after exercise is crucial for preventing overexercise.

One Last Thing . . .

You'll notice so many positive changes in yourself as you build these exercises into your routine, and I'd love it if you could help me get these benefits to more people.

By sharing your honest opinion of this book and a little about your own story, you'll show new readers where they can find everything they need to ensure their golden years are truly golden.

Thank you so much for your support.

Please use this QR code to link to Amazon reviews for
Safe and Effective Workouts for Seniors.

APPENDIX I

DYNAMIC (WARM-UP) STRETCHES

Dynamic (Warm-Up) Stretches Exercises

Perform warm-up exercises before the "Create Your Own Program" or the "Four Week Ageless Agility program."

Exercise	Muscle Group	Position	FIT FUN	Optional Equipment	Illustration	Instructions	Reps or Hold Time	Sets
March in Place		Standing				Chapter 11	1 rep = 3 min	5–10 sets
Squats		Standing				Chapter 11	1 rep = 1 squat	5–10 sets
Walking Lunge		Standing				Chapter 11	1 rep = 1 lunge	5–10 sets
Arm Circles		Standing			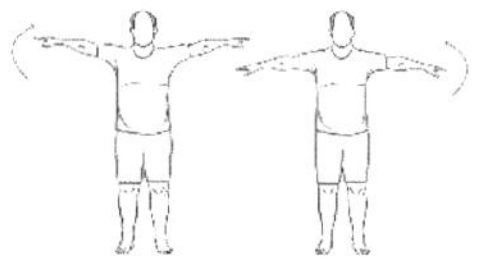	Chapter 11	1 rep = 90 seconds	5–10 sets
Shoulder Blade Squeeze		Standing				Chapter 11	1 rep = 1 squeeze	5–10 sets
Punches		Standing				Chapter 11	1 rep = 5-10 punches	5–10 sets

APPENDIX II

CREATE YOUR OWN EXERCISE PROGRAM

Create your own program from the following strength-building, flexibility, balance, and endurance exercises.

Strength Building – Upper Body

Exercise	Muscle Group	Position	FIT FUN	Optional Equipment	Illustration	Instructions	Reps or Hold Time	Sets
Shoulder Squeeze	Shoulders	Standing			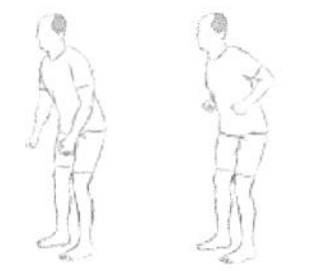	Chapter 10	10 reps	1–3 sets
Bicep Strengthening	Biceps	Standing				Chapter 10	10 reps	1–3 sets
Triceps Push	Triceps	Seated			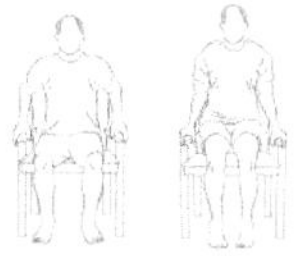	Chapter 10	Pause 3–5 secs in up position 10 reps	
Elbow Extensions	Elbow, Forearm, Wrists	Seated or Standing			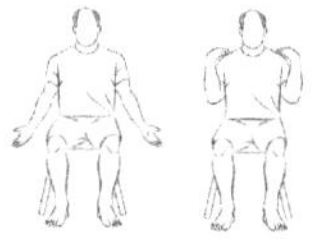	Chapter 10	10 reps	
Shoulder Raises	Shoulders	Seated			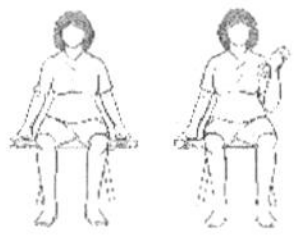	Chapter 10	10 reps	1–3 sets
Rotator Cuff Strengthen	Shoulder, Middle Back	Seated or Standing			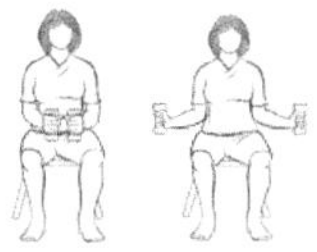	Chapter 10	10 reps	1–3 sets
Seated Push Back	Shoulder, Chest	Seated			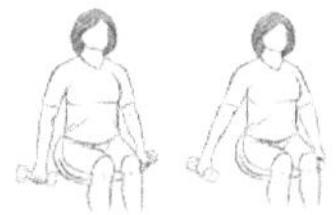	Chapter 10	10 reps	1–3 sets

Dumbbell Row	Shoulder, Middle Back	Kneeling				Chapter 10	10 reps	1–3 sets
Push Back	Shoulder, Chest, Middle Back	Kneeling				Chapter 10	10 reps	1–3 sets
Arm Lifts	Upper Back, Shoulders	Seated			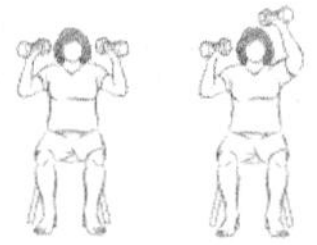	Chapter 10	10 reps	1–3 sets
Chest Extension	Chest	Seated			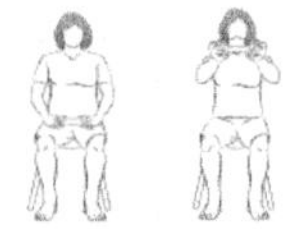	Chapter 10	10 reps	1–3 sets
Bicep Curl	Biceps	Seated			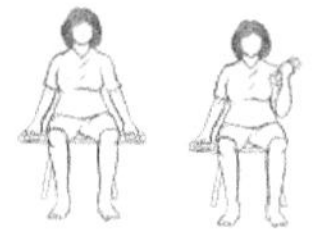	Chapter 10	10 reps	1–3 sets
Triceps Curl	Triceps	Seated			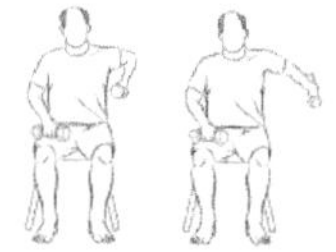	Chapter 10	10 reps	1–3 sets

Strength Building – Core

Exercise	Muscle Group	Position	FIT FUN	Optional Equipment	Illustration	Instructions	Reps or Hold Time	Sets
Diaphragmatic Breathing	Diaphragm	Seated or Lying Down			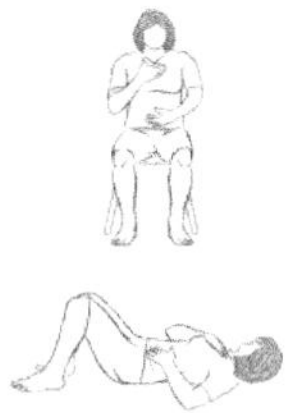	Chapter 10	Breathe for 5–6 minutes	3–4 times per day
Pelvic Floor Kegels	Pelvic Floor Muscles	Women: Standing or Lying Down Men: Seated or All Fours			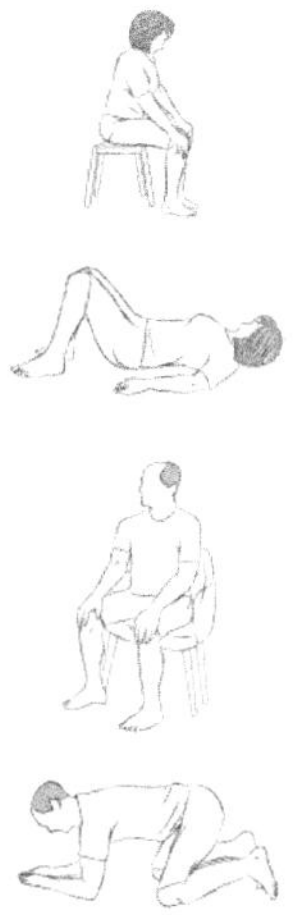	Chapter 10	Hold each Kegel 3–4 sec Rest Next Kegel	1 set is 2-3 Kegels 1–3 sets 2-3 times per day
Dolphin Kick	Abdomen	Lying Down			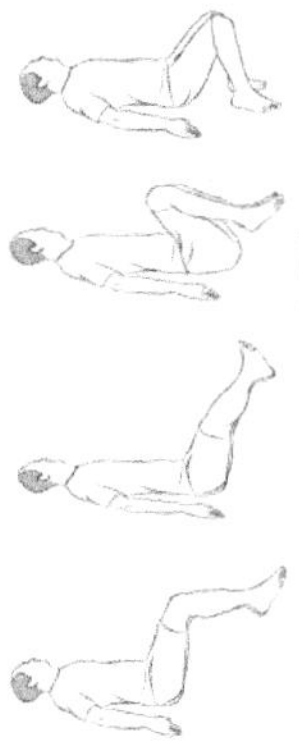	Chapter 10	10 reps	1–3 sets
Leg Extension	Abdomen	Lying Down			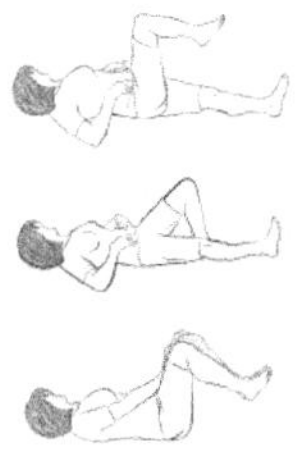	Chapter 10	10 reps	1–3 sets

Dead Bug	Abdomen	Lying Down				Chapter 10	10 reps	1–3 sets
Reverse Crunch	Abdomen	Lying Down				Chapter 10	10 reps	1–3 sets
Plank	Abdomen	Lying Down			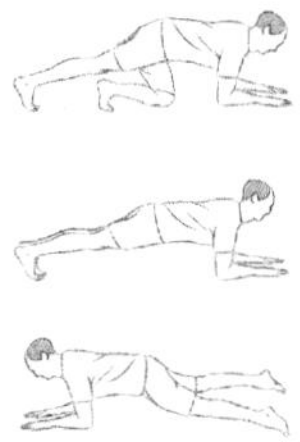	Chapter 10	10 reps	1–3 sets
Bridge	Lower Back, Glutes, Hips	Lying Down				Chapter 10	10 reps	1–3 sets
Extended Bridge	Lower Back, Glutes, Hips	Lying Down				Chapter 10	10 reps	1–3 sets
Clam	Hips	Lying Down			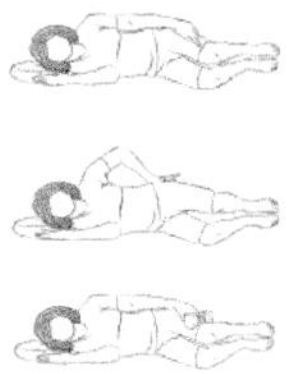	Chapter 10	10 reps	1–3 sets
Side Leg Lift	Hips	Lying Down			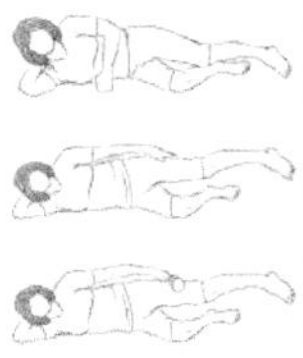	Chapter 10	10 reps	1–3 sets
Flutter Kick	Lower Back, Glutes, Hips	Lying Down			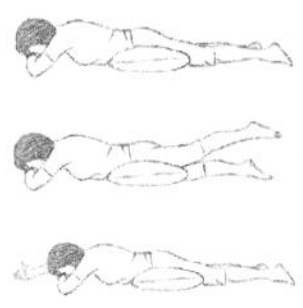	Chapter 10	10 reps	1–3 sets

Strength Building – Lower Body

Exercise	Muscle Group	Position	FIT FUN	Optional Equipment	Illustration	Instructions	Reps or Hold Time	Sets
Modified Heel Drops	Lower Back, Hips, Calves, Ankles	Standing			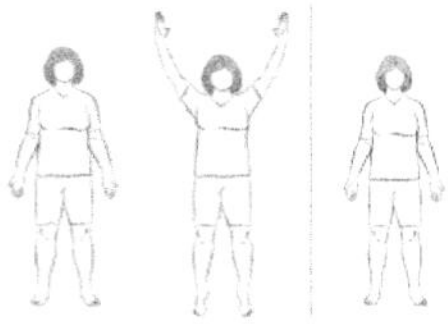	Chapter 10	10 reps	1–3 sets
Wall Squats	Thighs	Standing			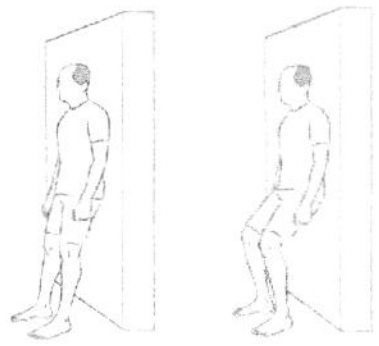	Chapter 10	10 reps	1–3 sets
Seated Leg Lifts	Thighs	Seated				Chapter 10	10 reps	1–3 sets
Standing Heel Raises	Thighs, Ankles, Feet	Standing				Chapter 10	10 reps	1–3 sets
Ankle Flex	Lower Legs, Ankles	Seated				Chapter 10	10 reps	1–3 sets
Rolling Ball Massage	Feet, Heels, Arches	Seated				Chapter 10	20 times	1–3 sets
Tiptoe Walking	Lower Legs (Calves and Shin), Ankles, and Toes	Standing			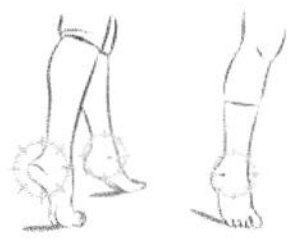	Chapter 10	5–15 min	1–3 times per day
Toe Grabs	Feet, Toes	Seated				Chapter 10	10 reps	1–3 sets

Inner Thigh Lifts	Thighs	Lying Down				Chapter 10	10 reps	1–3 sets
Outer Thigh Lifts	Thighs	Lying Down				Chapter 10	10 reps	1–3 sets
Seated March	Thighs, Lower Legs	Seated			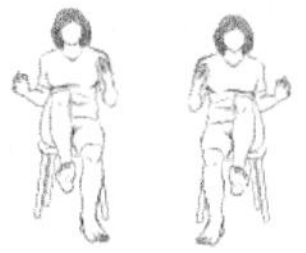	Chapter 10	10 reps	1–3 sets

Static Stretches – Upper Body

Exercise	Muscle Group	Position	FIT FUN	Optional Equipment	Illustration	Instructions	Reps or Hold Time	Sets
Neck Flex	Neck	Seated or Standing				Chapter 11	30 sec	1–3 sets
Neck Extension	Neck	Seated or Standing				Chapter 11	30 sec	1–3 sets
Neck Side Flexion	Neck	Seated or Standing				Chapter 11	30 sec	1–3 sets
Neck Rotation	Neck	Seated or Standing				Chapter 11	30 sec	1–3 sets
Chin Tuck	Neck	Seated or Standing			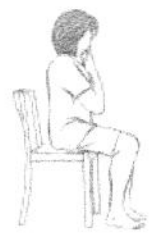	Chapter 11	5–7 sec hold 10 reps	1–7 sets
Shoulder Stretch	Shoulders	Seated or Standing				Chapter 11	30 sec	1–3 sets
Overhead Stretch	Shoulders	Seated or Standing				Chapter 11	30 sec	1–3 sets
Elbow Wrap Stretch	Shoulders, Chest	Standing				Chapter 11	30 sec	1–3 sets

Standing Chest Expansion	Shoulders	Standing				Chapter 11	30 sec	1–3 sets
Shoulder Shrug	Shoulders	Seated or Standing			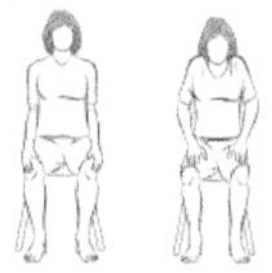	Chapter 11	10 sec shrug 10 reps	1–3 sets
Shoulder Pull	Shoulders	Seated				Chapter 11	30 sec	1–3 sets
Chest Expansion	Shoulders	Seated or Standing				Chapter 11	30 sec	1–3 sets
Upper Back Stretch	Upper Back	Seated				Chapter 11	30 sec	1–3 sets
Upper Back Extension	Upper Back	Seated			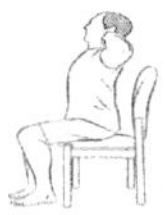	Chapter 11	30 sec	1–3 sets
Wrist and Forearm Flex Up/Down	Forearm, Wrists	Seated, Standing or Lying Down			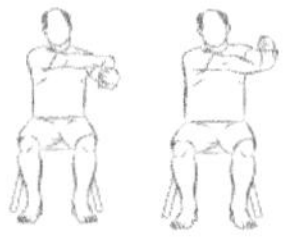	Chapter 11	30 sec	1–3 sets
Squeeze the Ball	Elbows, Wrists, Fingers	Seated, Standing or Lying Down				Chapter 11	30 sec	1–3 sets
Finger Spread	Fingers	Seated, Standing or Lying Down			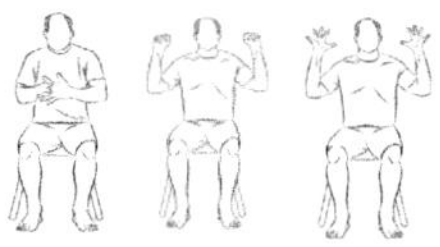	Chapter 11	5 sec hold, 10 reps	1–3 sets
Thumb Press	Fingers	Seated, Standing or Lying Down			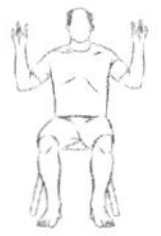	Chapter 11	30 sec	1–3 sets

Static Stretches – Lower Body

Exercise	Muscle Group	Position	FIT FUN	Optional Equipment	Illustration	Instructions	Reps or Hold Time	Sets
Lower Back Extension	Lower Back	Seated				Chapter 11	30 sec	1–3 sets
Lower Back Side Flex	Lower Back	Seated				Chapter 11	30 sec	1–3 sets
Seated Hamstring Stretch	Hamstrings	Seated			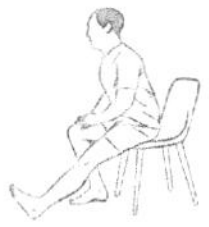	Chapter 11	30 sec	1–3 sets
Standing Quad Stretch	Quads	Standing				Chapter 11	30 sec	1–3 sets
Seated Glute Stretch	Glutes	Seated				Chapter 11	30 sec	1–3 sets
Seated Hip Stretch	Hips	Seated				Chapter 11	30 sec	1–3 sets
Standing Hip Stretch	Hips, Upper Legs	Standing				Chapter 11	30 sec	1–3 sets
Standing Calf Stretch	Calf, Back of Entire Leg	Standing				Chapter 11	30 sec	1–3 sets
Hamstring Stretch	Hamstrings	Lying Down				Chapter 11	30 sec	1–3 sets
Thigh Pull Stretch	Thighs, Upper Leg	Lying Down				Chapter 11	30 sec	1–3 sets
Figure Four Stretch	Upper Leg, Hips	Lying Down				Chapter 11	30 sec	1–3 sets

Balance Exercises

Exercise	Muscle Groups	Position	FIT FUN	Optional Equipment	Illustration	Instructions	Reps or Hold Time	Sets
Three-Way Toe Tap	Abdominals, Hips	Standing			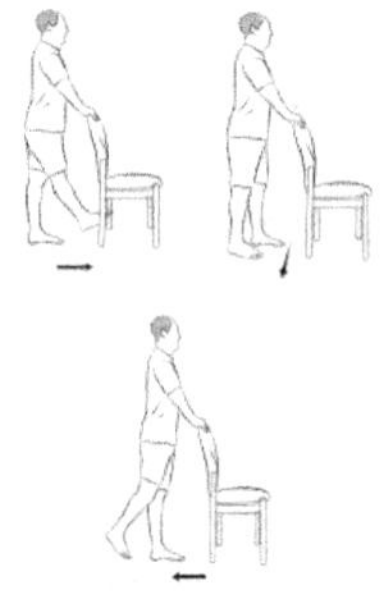	Chapter 12	10 reps	1–3 sets
Side to Side	Abdominals, Hips, Glutes, Quads, Lower Legs (Calves and Shin)	Standing				Chapter 12	10 reps	1–3 sets
Sit to Stand	Abdominals, Lower Back, Glutes, Quads, Hamstrings	Standing			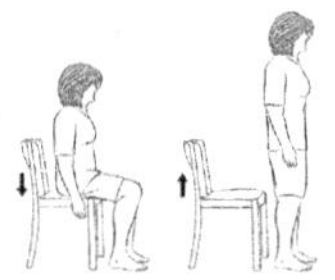	Chapter 12	10 reps	1–3 sets
Wall Press	Shoulders, Chest, Triceps, Abdominals, Glutes, Quads, Calves	Standing			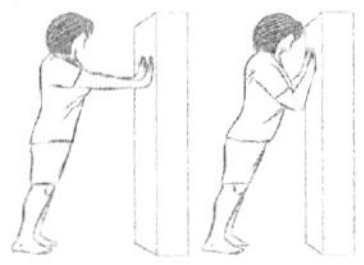	Chapter 12	10 reps	1–3 sets
Stand on One Foot	Abdominals, Quads, Hamstrings, Calves, Ankles	Standing			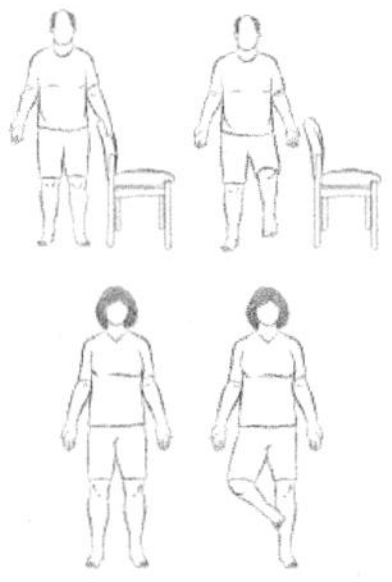	Chapter 12	10 reps	1–3 sets

Heel Raises	Calves, Ankles, Feet	Standing			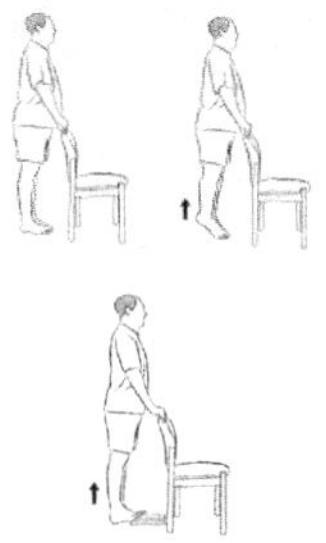	Chapter 12	10 reps	1–3 sets
Toe Raises	Calves, Ankles, Feet	Standing or Seated				Chapter 12	10 reps	1–3 sets

Endurance Building Exercises

Exercise	Muscle Group	Position	FIT FUN	Optional Equipment	Illustration	Instructions	Reps or Hold Time	Sets
Walking						Chapter 13		10–30 minutes
Cycling						Chapter 13		10–30 minutes
Swimming						Chapter 13		10–30 minutes
Dancing						Chapter 13		10–30 minutes

APPENDIX III

4-WEEK AGELESS AGILITY EXERCISE PROGRAMS

BEGINNERS

4-Week Ageless Agility Program

WEEK 1

Beginners Week 1 – Day 1

STRENGTH BUILDING	Bicep Curl	10 reps	1 set
	Triceps Curl	10 reps	1 set
	Chest Extension	10 reps	1 set
	Shoulder Raises	10 reps	1 set
	Rotator Cuff Strengthen	10 reps	1 set
	Seated Push Back	10 reps	1 set
	Diaphragmatic Breathing	Breathe for 5-6 minutes	3–4 times per day
	Dolphin Kick	10 reps	1 set
	Extended Bridge	10 reps	1 set
	Leg Extension	10 reps	1 set
	Clam	10 reps	1 set
	Outer Thigh Lifts	10 reps	1 set
	Seated Leg Lifts	10 reps	1 set
	Toe Grabs	10 reps	1 set
	Ankle Flex	10 reps	1 set
BALANCE	Heel Raises	10 reps	1 set
	Side to Side	10 reps	1 set
	Three-Way Toe Tap	10 reps	1 set

Beginners Week 1 – Day 2

FLEXIBILITY	Neck Extension	30 sec	1 set
	Neck Side Flexion	30 sec	1 set
	Chin Tuck	5–7 sec hold 10 reps	1 set
	Shoulder Shrug	10 sec shrug 10 reps	1 set
	Shoulder Stretch	30 sec	1 set
	Hamstring Stretch	30 sec	1 set
	Standing Calf Stretch	30 sec	1 set
	Standing Quad Stretch	30 sec	1 set

Beginners Week 1 – Day 3

FLEXIBILITY	Neck Extension	30 sec	1 set
	Neck Flex	30 sec	1 set
	Shoulder Shrug	10 sec shrug 10 reps	1 set
	Shoulder Stretch	30 sec	1 set
	Standing Chest Expansion	30 sec	1 set
	Lower Back Extension	30 sec	1 set
	Upper Back Extension	30 sec	1 set
	Standing Quad Stretch	30 sec	1 set
	Hamstring Stretch	30 sec	1 set
	Figure Four Stretch	30 sec	1 set
	Thigh Pull Stretch	30 sec	1 set
ENDURANCE	Walking		10–15 min

Beginners Week 1 – Day 4

BALANCE	Stand on One Foot	10 reps	1 set
	Wall Presses	10 reps	1 set
	Heel Raises	10 reps	1 set
	Toe Raises	10 reps	1 set

Beginners Week 1 – Day 5

STRENGTH BUILDING	Elbow Extensions	10 reps	1 set
	Arm Lifts	10 reps	1 set
	Seated Push Back	10 reps	1 set
	Shoulder Squeeze	10 reps	1 set
	Flutter Kick	10 reps	1 set
	Plank	10 reps	1 set
	Side Leg Lift	10 reps	1 set
	Wall Squats	10 reps	1 set
	Modified Heel Drops	10 reps	1 set
	Standing Heel Raises	10 reps	1 set
FLEXIBILITY	Neck Flex	30 sec	1 set
	Shoulder Shrug	10 sec shrug 10 reps	1 set
	Hamstring Stretch	30 sec	1 set
	Thigh Pull Stretch	30 sec	1 set

Beginners Week 1 – Day 6

ENDURANCE	Swimming		10–15 min

Beginners Week 1 – Day 7

FLEXIBILITY	Wrist and Forearm Flex Up/Down	30 sec	1 set
	Squeeze the Ball	30 sec	1 set
	Elbow Wrap Stretch	30 sec	1 set
	Finger Spread	30 sec	1 set
	Thumb Press	30 sec	1 set
BALANCE	Stand on One Foot	10 reps	1 set
	Heel Raises	10 reps	1 set
	Toe Raises	10 reps	1 set
	Sit to Stand	10 reps	1 set

BEGINNERS

4-Week Ageless Agility Program

WEEK 2

Beginners **Week 2 – Day 1**

STRENGTH BUILDING	Bicep Curl	10 reps	1 set
	Triceps Curl	10 reps	1 set
	Chest Extension	10 reps	1 set
	Shoulder Raises	10 reps	1 set
	Rotator Cuff Strengthen	10 reps	1 set
	Pelvic Floor Kegels	Hold each Kegel 3–4 sec Rest Next Kegel	1 set of 2-3 Kegels
	Dolphin Kick	10 reps	1 set
	Extended Bridge	10 reps	1 set
	Leg Extension	10 reps	1 set
	Clam	10 reps	1 set
	Outer Thigh Lifts	10 reps	1 set
	Seated Leg Lifts	10 reps	1 set
	Toe Grabs	10 reps	1 set
	Ankle Flex	10 reps	1 set
BALANCE	Sit to Stand	10 reps	2 sets
	Stand on One Foot	10 reps	2 sets
	Wall Presses	10 reps	2 sets

Beginners Week 2 – Day 2

FLEXIBILITY	Chest Expansion	30 sec	2 sets
	Standing Chest Expansion	30 sec	2 sets
	Upper Back Stretch	30 sec	2 sets
	Lower Back Extension	30 sec	2 sets
	Standing Quad Stretch	30 sec	2 sets
	Figure Four Stretch	30 sec	2 sets
	Thigh Pull Stretch	30 sec	2 sets
	Standing Calf Stretch	30 sec	2 sets

Beginners Week 2 – Day 3

FLEXIBILITY	Neck Side Flexion	30 sec	2 sets
	Chin Tuck	5–7 sec hold 10 reps	2 sets
	Neck Rotation	30 sec	2 sets
	Shoulder Pull	30 sec	2 sets
	Overhead Stretch	30 sec	2 sets
	Wrist and Forearm Up/Down	30 sec	2 sets
	Lower Back Side Flex	30 sec	2 sets
	Upper Back Extension	30 sec	2 sets
	Seated Glute Stretch	30 sec	2 sets
	Seated Hip Stretch	30 sec	2 sets
	Standing Hip Stretch	30 sec	2 sets
	Seated Hamstring Stretch	30 sec	2 sets
ENDURANCE	Walking		10–15 min

Beginners Week 2 – Day 4

BALANCE	Stand on One Foot	10 reps	2 sets
	Three-Way Toe Tap	10 reps	2 sets
	Sit to Stand	10 reps	2 sets
	Side to Side	10 reps	2 sets

Beginners Week 2 – Day 5

STRENGTH BUILDING	Bicep Strengthening	10 reps	1 set
	Triceps Push	10 reps	1 set
	Push Back	10 reps	1 set
	Dumbbell Row	10 reps	1 set
	Squeeze the Ball	10 reps	1 set
	Reverse Crunch	10 reps	1 set
	Bridge	10 reps	1 set
	Dead Bug	10 reps	1 set
	Seated March	10 reps	1 set
	Inner Thigh Lifts	10 reps	1 set
	Tiptoe Walking	5–15 min	1 time per day
	Rolling Ball Massage	20 times	1 set
FLEXIBILITY	Neck Extension	30 sec	2 sets
	Shoulder Stretch	30 sec	2 sets
	Hamstring Stretch	30 sec	2 sets
	Thigh Pull Stretch	30 sec	2 sets

Beginners Week 2 – Day 6

ENDURANCE	Dancing		10–15 min

Beginners Week 2 – Day 7

FLEXIBILITY	Neck Flex	30 sec	2 sets
	Neck Extension	30 sec	2 sets
	Shoulder Shrug	10 sec shrug 10 reps	2 sets
	Shoulder Stretch	30 sec	2 sets
	Chest Expansion	30 sec	2 sets
BALANCE STRENGTH	Toe Raises	10 reps	2 sets
	Ankle Flex	30 sec	2 sets
	Tiptoe Walking	5–15 min	2 sets

BEGINNERS

4-Week Ageless Agility Program

WEEK 3

Beginners Week 3 – Day 1

	Elbow Extensions	10 reps	2 sets
	Arm Lifts	10 reps	2 sets
	Seated Push Back	10 reps	2 sets
	Shoulder Squeeze	10 reps	2 sets
STRENGTH	Flutter Kick	10 reps	2 sets
BUILDING	Diaphragmatic Breathing	Hold 5–6 sec	2 sets
	Plank	10 reps	2 sets
	Side Leg Lift	10 reps	2 sets
	Wall Squats	10 reps	2 sets
	Modified Heel Drops	10 reps	2 sets
	Standing Heel Raises	10 reps	2 sets
	Heel Raises	10 reps	2 sets
BALANCE	Wall Press	10 reps	2 sets
	Toe Raises	10 times	2 sets

Beginners Week 3 – Day 2

FLEXIBILITY	Neck Side Flexion	30 sec	2 sets
	Neck Rotation	30 sec	2 sets
	Chin Tuck	5–7 sec hold 10 reps	2 sets
	Shoulder Pull	30 sec	2 sets
	Overhead Stretch	30 sec	2 sets
	Seated Glute Stretch	30 sec	2 sets
	Seated Hamstring Stretch	30 sec	2 sets
	Standing Calf Stretch	30 sec	2 sets

Beginners Week 3 – Day 3

FLEXIBILITY	Neck Extension	30 sec	2 sets
	Neck Flex	30 sec	2 sets
	Shoulder Shrug	10 sec shrug 10 reps	2 sets
	Shoulder Stretch	30 sec	2 sets
	Standing Chest Expansion	30 sec	2 sets
	Chest Expansion	30 sec	2 sets
	Lower Back Extension	30 sec	2 sets
	Upper Back Extension	30 sec	2 sets
	Hamstring Stretch	30 sec	2 sets
	Standing Quad Stretch	30 sec	2 sets
	Figure Four Stretch	30 sec	2 sets
	Thigh Pull Stretch	30 sec	2 sets

ENDURANCE	Cycling		10-15 min

Beginners   Week 3 – Day 4

BALANCE	Wall Press	10 reps	2 sets
	Heel Raises	10 reps	2 sets
	Toe Raises	10 reps	2 sets
	Three-Way Toe Tap	10 reps	2 sets

Beginners   Week 3 – Day 5

STRENGTH BUILDING	Bicep Strengthening	10 reps	2 sets
	Triceps Push	10 reps	2 sets
	Push Back	10 reps	2 sets
	Dumbbell Row	10 reps	2 sets
	Squeeze the Ball	10 reps	2 sets
	Reverse Crunch	10 reps	2 sets
	Bridge	10 reps	2 sets
	Dead Bug	10 reps	2 sets
	Seated March	10 reps	2 sets
	Inner Thigh Lifts	10 reps	2 sets
	Tiptoe Walking	5–15 minutes	2 sets
	Rolling Ball Massage	20 times	2 sets
FLEXIBILITY	Neck Side Flexion	30 sec	2 sets
	Neck Rotation	30 sec	2 sets
	Shoulder Pull	30 sec	2 sets

	Overhead Stretch	30 sec	2 sets
	Seated Glute Stretch	30 sec	2 sets
	Seated Hamstring Stretch	30 sec	2 sets

Beginners Week 3 – Day 6

ENDURANCE	Swimming		10–15 min

Beginners Week 3 – Day 7

FLEXIBILITY	Wrist and Forearm Flex Up/Down	30 sec	2 sets
	Lower Back Extension	30 sec	2 sets
	Upper Back Extension	30 sec	2 sets
	Neck Side Flexion	30 sec	2 sets
	Standing Heel Raises	30 sec	2 sets
	Rolling Ball Massage	20 reps	2 sets
	Seated Glute Stretch	30 sec	2 sets
	Seated Hamstring Stretch	30 sec	2 sets
	Seated Hip Stretch	30 sec	2 sets

BEGINNERS

4-Week Ageless Agility Program

WEEK 4

<u>Beginners</u> <u>Week 4 – Day 1</u>

STRENGTH BUILDING	Bicep Curl	10 reps	2 sets
	Triceps Curl	10 reps	2 sets
	Chest Extension	10 reps	2 sets
	Shoulder Raises	10 reps	2 sets
	Rotator Cuff Strengthen	10 reps	2 sets
	Elbow Extensions	10 reps	2 sets
	Pelvic Floor Kegels	Hold each Kegel 3–4 sec Rest Next Kegel	2 sets of 2-3 Kegels
	Dolphin Kick	10 reps	2 sets
	Extended Bridge	10 reps	2 sets
	Leg Extension	10 reps	2 sets
	Clam	10 reps	2 sets
	Outer Thigh Lifts	10 reps	2 sets
	Seated Leg Lifts	10 reps	2 sets
	Toe Grabs	10 reps	2 sets
	Ankle Flex	10 reps	2 sets

BALANCE	Toe Raises	10 reps	2 sets
	Side to Side	10 reps	2 sets
	Three-Way Toe Tap	10 reps	2 sets

Beginners Week 4 – Day 2

FLEXIBILITY	Wrist and Forearm Flex Up/Down	30 sec	2 sets
	Lower Back Side Flex	30 sec	2 sets
	Standing Chest Expansion	30 sec	2 sets
	Upper Back Extension	30 sec	2 sets
	Seated Hip Stretch	30 sec	2 sets
	Standing Hip Stretch	30 sec	2 sets
	Standing Calf Stretch	30 sec	2 sets

Beginners Week 4 – Day 3

FLEXIBILITY	Neck Side Flexion	30 sec	2 sets
	Neck Rotation	30 sec	2 sets
	Chin Tuck	5–7 sec hold 10 reps	2 sets
	Shoulder Pull	30 sec	2 sets
	Overhead Stretch	30 sec	2 sets
	Wrist and Forearm Flex Up/Down	30 sec	2 sets
	Lower Back Side Flex	30 sec	2 sets

	Upper Back Extension	30 sec	2 sets
	Seated Glute Stretch	30 sec	2 sets
	Seated Hamstring Stretch	30 sec	2 sets
	Standing Hip Stretch	30 sec	2 sets
	Seated Hip Stretch	30 sec	2 sets
ENDURANCE	Swimming		10–15 min

Beginners **Week 4 – Day 4**

BALANCE	Side to Side	10 reps	2 sets
	Three-Way Toe Tap	10 reps	2 sets
	Sit to Stand	10 reps	2 sets
	Stand on One Foot	10 reps	2 sets

Beginners **Week 4 – Day 5**

STRENGTH BUILDING	Elbow Extensions	10 reps	2 sets
	Arm Lifts	10 reps	2 sets
	Seated Push Back	10 reps	2 sets
	Shoulder Squeeze	10 reps	2 sets
	Flutter Kick	10 reps	2 sets
	Plank	10 reps	2 sets
	Side Leg Lift	10 reps	2 sets
	Wall Squats	10 reps	2 sets
	Modified Heel Drops	10 reps	2 sets
	Standing Heel Raises	10 reps	2 sets

FLEXIBILITY	Wrist and Forearm Flex Up/Down	30 sec	2 sets
	Lower Back Side Flex	30 sec	2 sets
	Upper Back Extension	30 sec	2 sets
	Seated Hip Stretch	30 sec	2 sets

Beginners Week 4 – Day 6

ENDURANCE	Cycling		10–15 min

Beginners Week 4 – Day 7

FLEXIBILITY	Neck Rotation	30 sec	2 sets
	Shoulder Pull	30 sec	2 sets
	Overhead Stretch	30 sec	2 sets
	Lower Back Side Flex	30 sec	2 sets
	Upper Back Extension	30 sec	2 sets
STRENGTH	Toe Grabs	10 reps	2 sets
	Rolling Ball	20 times	2 sets
	Tiptoe Walking	5–15 min	2 sets

INTERMEDIATE

4-Week Ageless Agility Program

WEEK 1

Intermediate Week 1 – Day 1

STRENGTH BUILDING	Bicep Curl	10 reps	1 set
	Triceps Curl	10 reps	1 set
	Chest Extension	10 reps	1 set
	Shoulder Raises	10 reps	1 set
	Rotator Cuff Strengthen	10 reps	1 set
	Seated Push Back	10 reps	1 set
	Diaphragmatic Breathing	Breathe for 5–6 minutes	3–4 times per day
	Dolphin Kick	10 reps	1 set
	Extended Bridge	10 reps	1 set
	Leg Extension	10 reps	1 set
	Clam	10 reps	1 set
	Outer Thigh Lifts	10 reps	1 set
	Seated Leg Lifts	10 reps	1 set
	Toe Grabs	10 reps	1 set
	Ankle Flex	10 reps	1 set
BALANCE	Heel Raises	10 reps	1 set
	Side to Side	10 reps	1 set
	Three-Way Toe-Tap	10 reps	1 set

Intermediate Week 1 – Day 2

FLEXIBILITY	Neck Extension	30 sec	1 set
	Neck Side Flexion	30 sec	1 set
	Chin Tuck	5–7 sec hold 10 reps	1 set
	Shoulder Shrug	10 sec shrug 10 reps	1 set
	Shoulder Stretch	30 sec	1 set
	Hamstring Stretch	30 sec	1 set
	Standing Calf Stretch	30 sec	1 set
	Standing Quad Stretch	30 sec	1 set
ENDURANCE	Walking		30 min

Intermediate Week 1 – Day 3

FLEXIBILITY	Bicep Strengthening	10 reps	1 set
	Triceps Push	10 reps	1 set
	Push Back	10 reps	1 set
	Dumbbell Row	10 reps	1 set
	Reverse Crunch	10 reps	1 set
	Bridge	10 reps	1 set
	Dead Bug	10 reps	1 set
	Seated March	10 reps	1 set
	Inner Thigh Lifts	10 reps	1 set
	Tiptoe Walking	5–15 min	1 set
	Rolling Ball Massage	20 times	1 set

ENDURANCE	Swimming		10–15 min

Intermediate Week 1 – Day 4

BALANCE	Stand on One Foot	10 reps	1 set
	Wall Press	10 reps	1 set
	Heel Raises	10 reps	1 set
	Toe Raises	10 reps	1 set

Intermediate Week 1 – Day 5

STRENGTH BUILDING	Elbow Extensions	10 reps	1 set
	Arm Lift	10 reps	1 set
	Seated Push Back	10 reps	1 set
	Shoulder Squeeze	10 reps	1 set
	Flutter Kick	10 reps	1 set
	Plank	10 reps	1 set
	Side Leg Lift	10 reps	1 set
	Wall Squats	10 reps	1 set
	Modified Heel Drops	10 reps	1 set
	Standing Heel Raises	10 reps	1 set
FLEXIBILITY	Neck Flex	30 sec	1 set
	Shoulder Shrug	10 sec shrug 10 reps	1 set
	Hamstring Stretch	30 sec	1 set
	Thigh Pull Stretch	30 sec	1 set

Intermediate Week 1 – Day 6

	Neck Extension	30 sec	1 set
	Neck Flex	30 sec	1 set
	Shoulder Shrug	10 sec shrugs 10 reps	1 set
	Standing Chest Expansion	30 sec	1 set
	Chest Expansion	30 sec	1 set
FLEXIBILITY	Lower Back Extension	30 sec	1 set
	Upper Back Extension	30 sec	1 set
	Hamstring Stretch	30 sec	1 set
	Standing Quad Stretch	30 sec	1 set
	Figure Four Stretch	30 sec	1 set
	Thigh Pull Stretch	30 sec	1 set
ENDURANCE	Walking		30 min

Intermediate Week 1 – Day 7

	Wrist and Forearm Flex Up/Down	30 sec	1 set
	Squeeze the Ball	30 sec	1 set
FLEXIBILITY	Elbow Wrap Stretch	30 sec	1 set
	Finger Spread	30 sec	1 set
	Thumb Press	30 sec	1 set
	Sit to Stand	10 reps	1 set
	Side to Side	10 reps	1 set
BALANCE	Three-Way Toe Tap	10 reps	1 set

	Stand on One Foot	10 reps	1 set
	Toe Raises	10 reps	1 set

INTERMEDIATE

4-Week Ageless Agility Program

WEEK 2

Intermediate Week 2 – Day 1

	Bicep Curl	10 reps	1 set
	Triceps Curl	10 reps	1 set
	Chest Extension	10 reps	1 set
	Shoulder Raises	10 reps	1 set
	Rotator Cuff Strengthen	10 reps	1 set
	Seated Push Back	10 reps	1 set
STRENGTH BUILDING	Diaphragmatic Breathing	Breathe for 5–6 minutes	1 set
	Dolphin Kick	10 reps	1 set
	Extended Bridge	10 reps	1 set
	Leg Extension	10 reps	1 set
	Clam	10 reps	1 set
	Outer Thigh Lifts	10 reps	1 set
	Seated Leg Lifts	10 reps	1 set
	Toe Grabs	10 reps	1 set
	Ankle Flex	10 reps	1 set
	Sit to Stand	10 reps	2 sets
BALANCE	Wall Press	10 reps	2 sets
	Stand on One Foot	10 reps	2 sets

Intermediate Week 2 – Day 2

FLEXIBILITY	Standing Chest Expansion	30 sec	2 sets
	Chest Expansion	30 sec	2 sets
	Lower Back Extension	30 sec	2 sets
	Upper Back Stretch	30 sec	2 sets
	Standing Quad Stretch	30 sec	2 sets
	Figure Four Stretch	30 sec	2 sets
	Thigh Pull Stretch	30 sec	2 sets
	Standing Calf Stretch	30 sec	2 sets
ENDURANCE	Cycling		30 min

Intermediate Week 2 – Day 3

STRENGTH BUILDING	Elbow Extensions	10 reps	1 set
	Arm Lifts	10 reps	1 set
	Seated Push Back	10 reps	1 set
	Shoulder Squeeze	10 reps	1 set
	Flutter Kick	10 reps	1 set
	Plank	10 reps	1 set
	Side Leg Lift	10 reps	1 set
	Wall Squats	10 reps	1 set
	Modified Heel Drops	10 reps	1 set
	Standing Heel Raises	10 reps	1 set
ENDURANCE	Walking		30 min

Intermediate Week 2 – Day 4

BALANCE	Stand on One Foot	10 reps	2 sets
	Three-Way Toe Tap	10 reps	2 sets
	Sit to Stand	10 reps	2 sets
	Sit to Stand	10 reps	2 sets

Intermediate Week 2 – Day 5

STRENGTH BUILDING	Bicep Strengthening	10 reps	1 set
	Triceps Curl	10 reps	1 set
	Push Back	10 reps	1 set
	Dumbbell Row	10 reps	1 set
	Reverse Crunch	10 reps	1 set
	Bridge	10 reps	1 set
	Dead Bug	10 reps	1 set
	Seated March	10 reps	1 set
	Inner Thigh Lifts	10 reps	1 set
	Tiptoe Walking	5–15 min	1 set
	Rolling Ball Massage	20 times	1 set
FLEXIBILITY	Neck Side Flexion	30 sec	2 sets
	Shoulder Stretch	30 sec	2 sets
	Hamstring Stretch	30 sec	2 sets
	Thigh Pull Stretch	30 sec	2 sets

Intermediate Week 2 – Day 6

FLEXIBILITY	Neck Side Flexion	30 sec	2 sets
	Chin Tuck	5–7 sec hold 10 reps	2 sets
	Neck Rotation	30 sec	2 sets
	Shoulder Pull	30 sec	2 sets
	Overhead Stretch	30 sec	2 sets
	Wrist and Forearm Flex Up/Down	30 sec	2 sets
	Lower Back Side Flex	30 sec	2 sets
	Upper Back Extension	30 sec	2 sets
	Seated Glute Stretch	30 sec	2 sets
	Seated Hamstring Stretch	30 sec	2 sets
	Seated Hip Stretch	30 sec	2 sets
	Standing Hip Stretch	30 sec	2 sets
ENDURANCE	Dancing		30 min

Intermediate Week 2 – Day 7

FLEXIBILITY	Neck Flex	30 sec	2 sets
	Neck Extension	30 sec	2 sets
	Shoulder Shrug	10 sec shrug 10 reps	2 sets
	Shoulder Stretch	30 sec	2 sets
	Chest Expansion	30 sec	2 sets

STRENGTH	Rolling Ball Massage	20 times	2 sets
	Ankle Flex	10 reps	2 sets
	Tiptoe Walking	10–15 min	2 sets

INTERMEDIATE

4-Week Ageless Agility Program

WEEK 3

<u>Intermediate</u> <u>Week 3 – Day 1</u>

	Elbow Extensions	10 reps	2 sets
	Arm Lifts	10 reps	2 sets
	Seated Push Back	10 reps	2 sets
	Shoulder Squeeze	10 reps	2 sets
STRENGTH	Flutter Kick	10 reps	2 sets
BUILDING	Diaphragmatic Breathing	Breathe for 5–6 minutes	3–4 times per day
	Plank	10 reps	2 sets
	Side Leg Lift	10 reps	2 sets
	Wall Squats	10 reps	2 sets
	Modified Heel Drops	10 reps	2 sets
	Standing Heel Raises	10 reps	2 sets
	Wall Press	10 reps	3 sets
BALANCE	Heel Raises	10 reps	3 sets
	Toe Raises	10 reps	3 sets

Intermediate Week 3 – Day 2

	Neck Side Flexion	30 sec	2 sets
	Neck Rotation	30 sec	2 sets
	Chin Tuck	5–7 sec hold 10 reps	2 sets
FLEXIBILITY	Shoulder Pull	30 sec	2 sets
	Overhead Stretch	30 sec	2 sets
	Seated Glute Stretch	30 sec	2 sets
	Seated Hamstring Stretch	30 sec	2 sets
	Standing Calf Stretch	30 sec	2 sets
ENDURANCE	Cycling		30 min

Intermediate Week 3 – Day 3

	Bicep Curl	10 reps	2 sets
	Triceps Curl	10 reps	2 sets
	Chest Extension	10 reps	2 sets
	Shoulder Raises	10 reps	2 sets
STRENGTH	Rotator Cuff Strengthen	10 reps	2 sets
BUILDING	Seated Push Back	10 reps	2 sets
	Shoulder Raises	Hold each Kegel 3–4 sec Rest Next Kegel	2 sets of 2-3 Kegels

	Rotator Cuff Strengthen	10 reps	2 sets
	Extended Bridge	10 reps	2 sets
	Leg Extension	10 reps	2 sets
	Clam	10 reps	2 sets
	Outer Thigh Lifts	10 reps	2 sets
	Seated Leg Lifts	10 reps	2 sets
	Toe Grabs	10 reps	2 sets
	Ankle Flex	10 reps	2 sets
ENDURANCE	Walking		30 min

Intermediate Week 3 – Day 4

BALANCE	Wall Press	10 reps	3 sets
	Heel Raises	10 reps	3 sets
	Toe Raises	10 reps	3 sets
	Three-Way Toe Tap	10 reps	3 sets

Intermediate Week 3 – Day 5

STRENGTH BUILDING	Bicep Strengthening	10 reps	2 sets
	Triceps Push	10 reps	2 sets
	Push Back	10 reps	2 sets
	Dumbbell Row	10 reps	2 sets
	Squeeze the Ball	10 reps	2 sets
	Reverse Crunch	10 reps	2 sets
	Bridge	10 reps	2 sets

	Dead Bug	10 reps	2 sets
	Seated March	10 reps	2 sets
	Inner Thigh Lifts	10 reps	2 sets
	Tiptoe Walking	5–15 min	2 sets
	Rolling Ball Massage	20 times	2 sets
FLEXIBILITY	Neck Side Flexion	30 sec	2 sets
	Neck Rotation	30 sec	2 sets
	Shoulder Pull	30 sec	2 sets
	Overhead Stretch	30 sec	2 sets
	Seated Glute Stretch	30 sec	2 sets
	Seated Hamstring Stretch	30 sec	2 sets

Intermediate Week 3 – Day 6

FLEXIBILITY	Neck Extension	30 sec	2 sets
	Neck Flex	30 sec	2 sets
	Shoulder Shrug	10 sec shrug 10 reps	2 sets
	Shoulder Stretch	30 sec	2 sets
	Standing Chest Expansion	30 sec	2 sets
	Chest Expansion	30 sec	2 sets
	Lower Back Extension	30 sec	2 sets
	Upper Back Extension	30 sec	2 sets
	Hamstring Stretch	30 sec	2 sets
	Standing Quad Stretch	30 sec	2 sets
	Figure Four Stretch	30 sec	2 sets
	Thigh Pull Stretch	30 sec	2 sets
ENDURANCE	Dancing		30 Min

Intermediate Week 3 – Day 7

FLEXIBILITY	Wrist and Forearm Flex Up/Down	30 sec	2 sets
	Lower Back Extension	30 sec	2 sets
	Upper Back Extension	30 sec	2 sets
	Neck Side Flexion	30 sec	2 sets
	Rolling Ball Massage	20 times	2 sets
	Seated Glute Stretch	30 sec	2 sets
	Seated Hamstring Stretch	30 sec	2 sets
	Seated Hip Stretch	30 sec	2 sets

INTERMEDIATE

4-Week Ageless Agility Program

WEEK 4

Intermediate Week 4 – Day 1

STRENGTH BUILDING	Bicep Curl	10 reps	2 sets
	Triceps Curl	10 reps	2 sets
	Triceps Curl	10 reps	2 sets
	Shoulder Raises	10 reps	2 sets
	Rotator Cuff Strengthen	10 reps	2 sets
	Seated Push Back	10 reps	2 sets
	Pelvic Floor Kegels	Hold each Kegel 3–4 sec Rest Next Kegel	2 sets of 2-3 Kegels
	Dolphin Kick	10 reps	2 sets
	Extended Bridge	10 reps	2 sets
	Leg Extension	10 reps	2 sets
	Clam	10 reps	2 sets
	Outer Thigh Lifts	10 reps	2 sets
	Seated Leg Lifts	10 reps	2 sets
	Toe Grabs	10 reps	2 sets
	Ankle Flex	10 reps	2 sets
	Toe Raises	10 reps	3 sets

BALANCE	Side to Side	10 reps	3 sets
	Three-Way Toe Tap	10 reps	3 sets

Intermediate Week 4 – Day 2

	Wrist and Forearm Flex Up/Down	30 sec	3 sets
	Lower Back Side Flex	30 sec	3 sets
	Standing Chest Expansion	30 sec	3 sets
FLEXIBILITY	Upper Back Extension	30 sec	3 sets
	Seated Hip Stretch	30 sec	3 sets
	Standing Hip Stretch	30 sec	3 sets
	Standing Calf Stretch	30 sec	3 sets
ENDURANCE	Walking		30 min

Intermediate Week 4 – Day 3

	Elbow Extensions	10 reps	2 sets
	Arm Lifts	10 reps	2 sets
	Seated Push Back	10 reps	2 sets
STRENGTH BUILDING	Shoulder Squeeze	10 reps	2 sets
	Flutter Kick	10 reps	2 sets
	Diaphragmatic Breathing	Breathe for 5–6 minutes	2 sets
	Plank	10 reps	2 sets
	Side Leg Lift	10 reps	2 sets

	Wall Squats	10 reps	2 sets
	Modified Heel Drops	10 reps	2 sets
	Standing Heel Raises	10 reps	2 sets
ENDURANCE	Cycling		30 min

Intermediate Week 4 – Day 4

BALANCE	Stand on One Foot	10 reps	3 sets
	Three-Way Toe Tap	10 reps	3 sets
	Side to Side	10 reps	3 sets
	Sit to Stand	10 reps	3 sets

Intermediate Week 4 – Day 5

STRENGTH BUILDING	Elbow Extensions	10 reps	2 sets
	Arm Lifts	10 reps	2 sets
	Seated Push Back	10 reps	2 sets
	Shoulder Squeeze	10 reps	2 sets
	Flutter Kick	10 reps	2 sets
	Plank	10 reps	2 sets
	Side Leg Lift	10 reps	2 sets
	Wall Squats	10 reps	2 sets
	Modified Heel Drops	10 reps	2 sets
	Standing Heel Raises	10 reps	2 sets
	Wrist and Forearm Flex Up/Down	30 sec	3 sets

	Wrist and Forearm Flex Up/Down	30 sec	3 sets
	Lower Back Side Flex	30 sec	3 sets
FLEXIBILITY	Upper Back Extension	30 sec	3 sets
	Seated Hip Stretch	30 sec	3 sets
	Standing Hip Stretch	30 sec	3 sets

Intermediate Week 4 – Day 6

	Neck Side Flexion	30 sec	3 sets
	Chin Tuck	5–7 sec hold 10 reps	3 sets
	Neck Rotation	30 sec	3 sets
	Shoulder Pull	30 sec	3 sets
	Overhead Stretch	30 sec	3 sets
FLEXIBILITY	Wrist and Forearm Flex Up/Down	30 sec	3 sets
	Lower Back Side Flex	30 sec	3 sets
	Upper Back Extension	30 sec	3 sets
	Seated Glute Stretch	30 sec	3 sets
	Seated Hamstring Stretch	30 sec	3 sets
	Seated Hip Stretch	30 sec	3 sets
	Standing Hip Stretch	30 sec	3 sets
ENDURANCE	Swimming		30 Min

Intermediate Week 4 – Day 7

FLEXIBILITY	Neck Rotation	30 sec	3 sets
	Shoulder Pull	30 sec	3 sets
	Overhead Stretch	30 sec	3 sets
	Lower Back Side Flex	30 sec	3 sets
	Upper Back Extension	30 sec	3 sets
STRENGTH	Standing Heel Raises	10 reps	3 sets
	Seated Leg Lifts	10 reps	3 sets
	Ankle Flex	10 reps	3 sets
	Tiptoe Walking	5–15 min	1–3 times per day

SOURCES

Abdominal Muscles Cleveland Clinic
https://my.clevelandclinic.org/health/body/21755-abdominal-muscles

How to Access Your Deep Core Muscles without Crunches [Video] YouTube
https://www.youtube.com/watch?v=8hSw74XqMAg.

14 of the best quotes about aging. Senior Planet
https://seniorplanet.org/14-of-the-best-quotes-about-aging/

Aerobic Activity for Older Adults
https://cphs.wayne.edu/occupational-therapy/resources/exercise_-_aerobic_activity_for_older_adults_1.pdf.

Aerobic Exercises for Seniors – Everything You Should Know Atulya Assisted Living
https://www.athulyaliving.com/blogs/aerobic-exercises-for-seniors-everything-you-should-know.php.

The Anatomy of your Abdominal Muscles Calibre
https://caliberstrong.com/blog/abdominal-muscles/.

Ankles – Bones, Ligaments, Muscles & Conditions Twin Boro Physical Therapy
https://twinboro.com/body/ankle/ankle-conditions-new-jersey.html.

(2014, May 14) Arthritis and Exercise: What to do and What Not to Do Mount Sinai
https://health.mountsinai.org/blog/arthritis-and-exercise-what-to-do-and-what-not-to-do/.

Balance Exercises Mayo Clinic
https://www.mayoclinic.org/healthy-lifestyle/fitness/multimeia/balance-exercises/sls-20076853?s=3.

(2022, September 19) *The Benefits of Balance Exercises for Older Adults*
https://www.edgemeredallas.com/blog/the-benefits-of-balance-exercises-for-older-adults/.

Best Ankle Weights for Seniors
https://elderstrength.com/best-ankle-weights-for-seniors/.

(2015, September 15) The Biceps Brachii Muscle Yoganatomy
https://www.yoganatomy.com/the-biceps-brachii-muscle/.

Davis, N (2020, May 29) *If You Aren't Breathing Like This, you're Sabotaging Your Workout* Healthline
https://www.healthline.com/health/fitness-exercise/when-to-inhale-and-exhale-during-exercise#How-to-breathe-for-maximum-efficiency.

Card, R & Bordoni, B (2022, February 27) *Anatomy, Bony Pelvis and Lower Limb, Foot Muscles* Nationals Library of Medicine
https://www.ncbi.nlm.nih.gov/books/NBK539705/.

Catlett, D (2017, November 7) *The Core: What is It?* Performance Course
https://medium.com/performance-course/the-core-what-is-it-98922c9cc384.

Cavaliere, J *How to Fix Low Back Pain Instantly* Axe Athlean-X
https://athleanx.com/articles/how-to-fix-low-back-pain-instantly.

Chandler, B *How to Measure Fitness at 70 years of age* AZ Central
https://healthyliving.azcentral.com/measure-fitness-70-years-age-18428.html.

The Complete Guide to Upper Body Muscles for Beginners Empower your wellness
https://www.empoweryourwellness.online/upper-body-muscles/#0-deltoid.

Core Wikipedia
https://en.wikipedia.org/wiki/Core_(anatomy).

Cristol, H (2021, March 26) *Posture Changes in Older Adults* Compass by WebMD
https://www.webmd.com/healthy-aging/features/posture-changes-older-adults.

Cronkleton, E (2020, May 11) *11 Balance Exercises for Seniors* Healthline
https://www.healthline.com/health/exercise-fitness/balance-exercises-for-seniors.

Cronkleton, E (2022, January 25) *13 Forearm Exercises to Do at the Gym or at Home* Healthline
https://www.healthline.com/health/forearm-exercises.

Cross, N Proper Dumbbell Weights for Older Men
https://healthyliving.azcentral.com/proper-dumbbell-weights-older-man-19225.html.

(2015, November) Current Concepts in Periodization of Strength and Conditioning for the Sports Physical Therapist National Library of Medicine
https://www.ncbi.nlm.nih.gov/pmc/articles/PMC4637911/#.

(2021, November 3) Daily Activities that Trigger Back Pain The Spine and Diagnostic Pain Treatment
https://www.spinediagnostic.com/blog/daily-activities-that-trigger-back-pain/.

Davis, T (2021, March 1) What Is a Vision Board and Why Make One? Psychology Today
https://www.psychologytoday.com/us/blog/click-here-happiness/202103/what-is-vision-board-and-why-make-one.

Davison, K How to Engage the Transversus Abdominis, and Why It's Important Healthline
https://www.healthline.com/health/fitness-exercise/transverse-abdominal-exercises#exercises.

Deltoid Physiopedia
https://www.physio-pedia.com/Deltoid.

Deering, S (2020, June 30) Back Pain Symptoms, Causes, Diagnosis and Treatment Health Central
https://www.spineuniverse.com/wellness/mobility/5-ways-strengthen-your-balance-prevent-spinal-fractures.

Disability and Sport: How a Little Exercise can have a Big Impact Disability Horizons
https://disabilityhorizons.com/2017/07/disability-and-sport-how-a-little-exercise-can-have-a-big-impact/#:~:text=muscle%20wastage%20due%20to%20difficulty,and%20trouble%20doing%20everyday%20movements.

(2016, March 15) Dynamic Stretching Versus Static Stretching UW Health
https://www.uwhealth.org/news/dynamic-stretching-versus-static-stretching.

Effects of Aging on Hand Function Physiopedia
https://www.physio-pedia.com/Effects_of_Ageing_on_Hand_Function.

Effects of Osteoarthritis on Quality of Life in Elderly Population of Bhubaneswar, India National Library of Medicine
https://www.ncbi.nlm.nih.gov/pmc/articles/PMC4647192/.

Elderly Flexibility Exercises for Seniors: We Need to Stretch for our Elderly Flexibility ElderGym Fitness for Seniors at Home
https://eldergym.com/elderly-flexibility/.

EnhanceFitness CDC
https://www.cdc.gov/prc/study-findings/research-briefs/senior-center-exercise-program-older-adults-enhancefitness.htm.

(2021, February 25) Exercise can boost your memory and thinking skills Mind and Mood
https://www.health.harvard.edu/mind-and-mood/exercise-can-boost-your-memory-and-thinking-skills.

Exercise helps Ease Arthritis pain and Stiffness Mayo Clinic
https://www.mayoclinic.org/diseases-conditions/arthritis/in-depth/arthritis/art-20047971.

Exercises Without Knee Pain Atulya Assisted Living
https://www.athulyaliving.com/blogs/exercises-without-knee-pain.php.

Fetters, K (2021, June 18) 11 Benefits of Strength Training That Have Nothing to Do with Muscle Size US News
https://health.usnews.com/wellness/fitness/articles/benefits-of-strength-training-that-have-nothing-to-do-with-muscle-size.

Fetters, K (2020, September 30) *12 Best Equipment-Free Strength Exercises for Older Adults* US News
https://health.usnews.com/health-news/health-wellness/articles/best-equipment-free-strength-exercises-for-older-adults.

The Fitness Hub Bailey Fitness
https://www.baileyfitness.com.au/blog/need-know-pectorals/.

Fitness: Tips for staying motivated Mayo Clinic
https://www.mayoclinic.org/healthy-lifestyle/fitness/in-depth/fitness/art-20047624.

5 Times When you Should Skip Your Workout and Take a Rest Day Better by Today
https://www.nbcnews.com/better/lifestyle/5-times-when-you-shouldn-t-work-out-ncna1068281.

Ford, D Dr (2018, November 21) Dealing with Common Aches and Pains as We Age With Dr. Donald Ford Cleveland Clinic
https://my.clevelandclinic.org/podcasts/health-essentials/dealing-with-common-aches-and-pains-as-we-age-with-dr-donald-ford.

The Four Pillars of an Effective Senior Fitness Program NYC Nutritionist
https://www.nycnutritionist.net/four-pillars-of-senior-fitness-program/#.

Four Types of Exercise Can Improve Your Health and Physical Ability National Institute on Aging
https://www.nia.nih.gov/health/four-types-exercise-can-improve-your-health-and-physical-ability.

Garnsey, M Osteoporosis vs Osteopenia: Facts to Know EntirelyHealth
https://entirelyhealth.com/conditions/osteoporosis/osteoporosis-vs-osteopenia-facts-to-know/.

Giving, O (2023, February 13) The Role of Your Abdominals in Everyday Life Tone Knowledge
https://www.tonepilates.ca/blog/the-role-of-your-abdominals-in-everyday-life/.

Gopez, J (2017, October 11) Exercise and Back Pain Spine Health
https://www.spine-health.com/wellness/exercise/exercise-and-back-pain.

Gorman, F What is the Difference Between Stretching in the Warm-up and the Cool-down AZ Central
https://healthyliving.azcentral.com/difference-between-stretching-warmup-cooldown-12912.html.

Hand, Wrist & Elbow Exercises for Seniors More Life Health [Video] YouTube
https://www.youtube.com/watch?v=MB-2Qa8lYqQ.

(2021, June 29) Health Benefits of Stretching for Older Adults Life Span
https://www.lifespanfitness.com/blogs/news/health-benefits-of-stretching-for-older-adults.

Healthy Lifestyle, Healthy Aging Mayo Clinic
https://www.mayoclinic.org/healthy-lifestyle/healthy-aging/in-depth/aging/art-20046070.

Help! I've Fallen and Can't Get Up! Please, Can Someone Help Me
https://www.neurobalancetherapy.org/transcript.

Hensen, B; et al (2022, August 25) Anatomy, Back, Muscles National Library of Medicine
https://www.ncbi.nlm.nih.gov/books/NBK537074/.

Holloway, B (2021, November) The Muscles of the Back Good Path
https://www.goodpath.com/learn/muscles-back.

(2022, June 30) How Can Strength Training Build Healthier Bodies as We Age National Institute on Aging
https://www.nia.nih.gov/news/how-can-strength-training-build-healthier-bodies-we-age#muscle.

How Many Muscles Are in the Human Body
https://www.healthline.com/health/how-many-muscles-are-in-the-human-body#muscle-facts,

How Much Physical Activity do Older Adults Need? CDC
https://www.cdc.gov/physicalactivity/basics/older_adults/index.htm.

How to do Kegel Exercises for Men Advanced Urology
https://advancedurology.com/advanced-blogging/how-to-do-kegel-exercises-for-men/.

Huetter, R (2020, May 04) Seniors' Top 10 Fears of Aging: Senior Living 101 Daystar Retirement Village
https://info.daystarseattle.com/senior-living-blog/understanding-your-aging-parents-seniors-top-10-fears.

Hussle (2020, August 7) Should You do the Same Workout Every Day Hussle
https://www.hussle.com/blog/should-you-do-the-same-workout-every-day/.

Is Lactic Acid Buildup Really What Causes Muscle Soreness After a Workout? Houston Methodist Leading Medicine
https://www.houstonmethodist.org/blog/articles/2021/oct/is-lactic-acid-buildup-really-what-causes-muscle-soreness-after-a-workout/#:~:text=%22Muscle%20soreness%20occurs%20because%20muscle,stronger%20during%20this%20repair%20process.%22

Kapoor, A (2021, April 18) Muscles Endurance Training for Seniors: 10 Important Reasons and Benefits LinkedIn
https://www.linkedin.com/pulse/muscular-endurance-training-seniors-10-important-reasons-kapoor#:.

Kemp, S (2019, February 14) Exercises to Improve Digestion Axa Health
https://www.axahealth.co.uk/health-information/gut-health/exercises-to-improve-digestion/.

Kerrigan, D Reduced Hip Extension During Walking: Healthy Elderly and Fallers versus Young Adults PubMed
https://pubmed.ncbi.nlm.nih.gov/11239282/.

Knee and Thigh Strengthening Progressive Physical Therapy and Rehabilitation Orange County Calif [Video] YouTube
https://www.youtube.com/watch?v=N2ukHIBBFAA.

Kutcher, M (2019, November 14) All About Walking: How to Walk More Without Pain More Life Health
https://morelifehealth.com/articles/walkingforseniors#1.

Kutcher, M A Month with Mike – An Exercise Program for Over 60's
https://drive.google.com/file/d/1Y5tkdSoRrp7ukVaziUlgATilqr-qJw_s/view?usp=sharing

Kutcher, M (2019, July 1) Regaining Flexibility After 60 – a Step by Step Guide More Life Health
https://morelifehealth.com/articles/regaining-flexibility-guide#3.

Kutcher, M (2020, December 22) What is the Pelvic Floor? More Life Health
https://morelifehealth.com/articles/pelvic-floor#1.

LaPlace, L (2021, March 15) Anatomy Lesson: The Hips and Glutes Our Center for Stability and Weight-bearing Goodwin Living
https://goodwinliving.org/blog/anatomy-lesson-the-hips-and-glutes/.

(2019, February 11) Level Up Your Workouts with Interval Training The YMCA
https://www.ymcasd.org/about-y/news-center/health/level-your-workouts-interval-training.

Lovell, K (2021, June 23) How to Avoid Losing Height as You Age Spine Universe
https://www.spineuniverse.com/wellness/avoid-height-loss-as-you-age.

Lower Muscles of the Back Anatomy and Low Back Pain Jacksonville Orthopaedic Institute
https://www.joionline.net/trending/content/lower-back-anatomy-and-low-back-pain.

Lumbar Spine Cleveland Clinic
https://my.clevelandclinic.org/health/articles/22396-lumbar-spine.

Making a Commitment to Exercise Optum
https://www.optum.com/library/health-wellness/.hub.fitness-tips.html.

MedlinePlus National Library of Medicine
https://medlineplus.gov/ency/article/004015.htm#:~:text=Muscles%20may%20become%20rigid%20with,tone%2C%20even%20with%20regular%20exercise.&text=Bones%20become%20more%20brittle%20and,pain%2C%20stiffness%2C%20and%20deformity.

Meyler, Z (2018, September 10) Easy Chin Tucks for Neck Pain Spine Health
https://www.spine-health.com/wellness/exercise/easy-chin-tucks-neck-pain.

Mid-Back Strain
https://www.suburbanortho.com/wp-content/uploads/2017/03/Mid-Back-Strain.pdf.

Millar, A Pelvic Floor Strong
https://drive.google.com/file/d/1X57rVpy5a6P2x8Q5wF2hbMjXuSzNMhtb/view?usp=sharing.

Miller, A Warm-up exercises for the elderly AZ Central
https://healthyliving.azcentral.com/warmup-exercises-elderly-9986.html.

A Month with Mike
https://drive.google.com/file/d/1Y5tkdSoRrp7ukVaziUlgATilqr-qJw_s/view?usp=sharing.

Morris, K Exercising Dangers for Obese People LiveStrong.com
https://www.livestrong.com/article/554136-exercising-dangers-for-obese-people/.

Muscles of the Back Good Path
https://www.goodpath.com/learn/muscles-back.

Muscles Strains in the Thigh Ortho Info
https://orthoinfo.aaos.org/en/diseases--conditions/muscle-strains-in-the-thigh/.

If My Knee Hurts, Why Exercise? OrthInfo
https://orthoinfo.aaos.org/en/staying-healthy/knee-exercises/.

National Institute on Aging
https://www.nia.nih.gov/health/how-older-adults-can-get-started-exercise.

Olbinsky, L (2020, July 17) Ten Amazing benefits of stretching Sworkit
https://sworkit.com/workouts/10-benefits-of-stretching.

Osteoarthritis (OA) Centers for Disease Control and Prevention
https://www.cdc.gov/arthritis/basics/osteoarthritis.htm.

Papalia, G et al (2020, August 11) The Effects of Physical Exercise on Balance and Prevention of Falls in Older People: A Systematic Review and Meta-Analysis National Library of Medicine
https://www.ncbi.nlm.nih.gov/pmc/articles/PMC7466089/#:~:text=There%20is%20overwhelming%20evidence%20that,reduction%2C%20and%20improving%20balance%20control.
Parrish, R *Normal Pulse After Three Minutes of Workout* AZ Central
https://healthyliving.azcentral.com/measure-fitness-70-years-age-18428.html.

Pelvic Floor Better Health Channel
https://www.betterhealth.vic.gov.au/health/conditionsandtreatments/pelvic-floor.

Pelvic Floor Muscles Continence Foundation of Australia
https://www.continence.org.au/about-continence/continence-health/pelvic-floor.

Physical Activity for Arthritis Centers for Disease Control and Prevention
https://www.cdc.gov/arthritis/basics/physical-activity-overview.html.

Physical Activity Guidelines for Adults Aged 19 to 64 NHS
https://www.nhs.uk/live-well/exercise/exercise-guidelines/physical-activity-guidelines-for-adults-aged-19-to-64/.

Physical Activity Guidelines for Older Adults NHS
https://www.nhs.uk/live-well/exercise/exercise-guidelines/physical-activity-guidelines-older-adults/.

Physio Neck and Shoulder Stretches [Video] YouTube
https://www.youtube.com/watch?v=ew3t1XiXLAk.

Plumbo, G (2012, September 20) Core Muscle strength- Why it's Important to Maintain Mayo Clinic
https://newsnetwork.mayoclinic.org/discussion/core-muscle-strength-why-its-important-to-maintain/.

Princey, A.J (2021, October 1) Significance of Using Fitness Equipment to Improve Results Post Workout Research Dive
https://www.researchdive.com/blog/significance-of-using-fitness-equipment-to-improve-results-post-workout..

Ramin, S, Adam (2019, August 26) How Exercise Benefits Urological Health U.S. News
https://health.usnews.com/health-care/for-better/articles/how-exercise-benefits-urological-health.

Revive your body's ability to Feel Strong, Stable and Balanced Neuro-balance therapy handbook – google docs
https://drive.google.com/file/d/1i93GMAs1XzJULLcLH3zD14DWmQfR5u9v/view?usp=sharing.

Santos-Longhurst, A (2018, July 30) Diaphragm Overview Healthline
https://www.healthline.com/human-body-maps/diaphragm#anatomy-and-function.

Scioscia. T (2017, August 24) Back Muscles and Low Back Pain Spine Health
https://www.spine-health.com/conditions/spine-anatomy/back-muscles-and-low-back-pain.

Senior exercise and fitness tips HelpGuide
https://www.helpguide.org/articles/healthy-living/exercise-and-fitness-as-you-age.htm.

Seguin, R.A et al Strength Training for Older Adults CDC
https://www.cdc.gov/physicalactivity/downloads/growing_stronger.pdf.

6 Exercises to Kill Chronic Knee, Foot or Hip Pain [Video] YouTube
https://www.youtube.com/watch?v=VrSGBwQGuMQ.

6 Scientifically proven obesity treatment options to manage weight Truth about weight
https://www.truthaboutweight.global/global/en/managing-your-weight/ manage-weight-6-scientifically-proven-obesity-treatment-options.html?cid= pse-ga-sea-tx-tawg&gclid=Cj0KCQiA2-2eBhClARIsAGLQ2Rn7VV4QFCrLFu-8Rd2ObbKCCrueol_6NjFW_tsCDbxfQwaY3eSqXYUaAus5EALw wcB

Smith, P.J Dr How Exercise Benefits Seniors and Aging Adults – Part 1
https://orthosurgeon.co.za/how-exercise-benefits-seniors-and-aging-adults/?gclid=Cj0KCQiA8t2eBhDeARIsAAVEga1wTN4n6rAIDM7ThGBoJS087GBQXVVU9-hvCAYc4rbV2oWpAZjAQV4aAq0BEALw wcB.

Standing Stretches for Seniors - Full Body 6 Stretches [Video] YouTube
https://www.youtube.com/watch?v=4hMWDxZB8WM&t=27s.

Stretching Exercises for Seniors - Upper Body & Lower Body Stretches for Seniors More Life Health [Video] YouTube
https://www.youtube.com/watch?v=eJbZHcB3mpE.

(2011, December 14) Sweden's news in English
https://www.thelocal.se/20111214/37944/.

Thigh Muscle Strength Exercise [Video] YouTube
https://www.youtube.com/watch?v=L9YgJpaDHjI.

13 Best Stretches for Seniors that can be Done Standing or seated Set for Set
https://www.setforset.com/blogs/news/stretches-for-seniors.

Tips For exercising with RA MedicalNewsToday
https://www.medicalnewstoday.com/articles/322917#exercise-tips.

Tips For Staying Healthy University of California San Francisco
https://www.ucsfhealth.org/education/tips-for-staying-healthy.

Waehner, A (2020, November 24) Cardio Exercises for Seniors Very Well Fit
https://www.verywellfit.com/cardio-exercise-guidelines-for-seniors-1230952.

Watson, M Best Exercise Equipment for Seniors Caring Senior Service
https://www.caringseniorservice.com/blog/exercise-equipment-for-seniors#:.

What Causes Bone Loss? National Library of Medicine
https://medlineplus.gov/ency/patientinstructions/000506.htm.

What is the Elderly Mobility Scale (EMS)? FreedomCare
https://freedomcare.com/elderly-mobility-scale/#:~:text=The%20elderly%20mobility%20scale%20(EMS)%20is%20a%20standardized%20test%20used,improving%20mobility%20in%20frail%20seniors.

Why Quality of Life Matters to Our Seniors Safe and Sound Home Care
https://safeandsoundhomecare.com/in-home-caregivers/why-quality-of-life-matters-to-our-seniors/#:~:text=The%20reason%20quality%2Dof%2Dlife, for%20their%20elderly%20loved%20ones

Your Big Why: What It Is and How to Find It Dolinski Group
https://dolinskigroup.com/agent-tips/your-big-why.

(2011, December) *You're Never Too Old – Keep Active as you Age* News in Health
https://newsinhealth.nih.gov/2011/12/youre-never-too-old#:~:text=We've%20all%20heard%20that,life%20in%20so%20many%20ways.

MY GIFT TO YOU!

Just My Way of Saying Thank You

Completely FREE

Scan the QR Code Below to Download

https://fallproof.aweb.page/

Printed in Great Britain
by Amazon

61382884R00185